Winning ROLLER HOCKEY

• Techniques • Tactics • Training •

Dave Easter
Head Coach
Canadian Men's National In-Line Hockey Team

Vern Stenlund
Director, Program Development
Huron Hockey School

HURON
Hockey School

Human Kinetics

We would like to express our thanks to our photographers, Gerry Marentette and Leslie Ellam; to Ken Houle and his family who operate the premier organization, the Detroit Roller Hockey Association, out of the Joe Dumars Field House, a world-class facility in Shelby Township, Michigan, we thank you for allowing us in to do a photo shoot—and we thank you for your encouragement and kindness. Finally, to all the people at Human Kinetics, a sincere thank you, especially to Elaine Mustain, Susan Moore-Kruse, and Ted Miller.

Library of Congress Cataloging-in-Publication Data

Easter, Dave, 1960-
    Winning roller hockey / Dave Easter, Vern Stenlund.
        p.   cm.
    ISBN 0-88011-657-9
    1. Roller hockey.   I. Stenlund, K. Vern.   II. Title.
    GV859.7.E27   1997   96-46412
    796.21--dc21   CIP

ISBN: 0-88011-657-9

Developmental Editor: Elaine Mustain; **Assistant Editor:** Susan Moore-Kruse; **Editorial Assistant:** Amy Carnes; **Copyeditor:** John Wentworth; **Proofreader:** Erin Cler; **Graphic Designer:** Stuart Cartwright; **Graphic Artist:** Yvonne Winsor; **Photo Editor:** Boyd LaFoon; **Cover Designer:** Jack Davis; **Photographer (cover):** Courtesy of I-TECH/Essy Ghavameddini; **Photographers (interior):** Gerry Marentette and Leslie Ellam; **Mac Artist:** Jennifer Delmotte; **Printer:** United Graphics

Human Kinetics books are available at special discounts for bulk purchase. Special editions or book excerpts can also be created to specification. For details, contact the Special Sales Manager at Human Kinetics.

Printed in the United States of America   10 9 8 7 6 5 4 3 2

Human Kinetics
Web site: www.humankinetics.com

United States: Human Kinetics
P.O. Box 5076
Champaign, IL 61825-5076
800-747-4457
e-mail: humank@hkusa.com

Canada: Human Kinetics
475 Devonshire Road, Unit 100
Windsor, ON N8Y 2L5
800-465-7301 (in Canada only)
e-mail: hkcan@mnsi.net

Europe: Human Kinetics
P.O. Box IW14
Leeds LS16 6TR, United Kingdom
+44 (0) 113 278 1708
e-mail: humank@hkeurope.com

Australia: Human Kinetics
57A Price Avenue
Lower Mitcham, South Australia 5062
08 8277 1555
e-mail: liahka@senet.com.au

New Zealand: Human Kinetics
P.O. Box 105-231, Auckland Central
09-523-3462
e-mail: hkp@ihug.co.nz

c o n t e n t s

Preface   iv
Key to Drills   v
Drill Finder   vi

Chapter 1 Getting Started   **1**

Chapter 2 Equipment   **9**

Chapter 3 Conditioning and Safety   **17**

Chapter 4 Skating   **35**

Chapter 5 Controlling the Puck   **57**

Chapter 6 Passing and Receiving   **81**

Chapter 7 Shooting   **105**

Chapter 8 Goaltending   **129**

Chapter 9 Offensive Team Strategies   **153**

Chapter 10 Transition Strategies   **173**

Chapter 11 Defensive Team Strategies   **185**

Chapter 12 Game Performance Tips   **205**

Sample Practice Plans   210
About the Authors   214

preface

Roller hockey is on a roll! From youth league players all the way up to professional ranks, roller hockey has become one of the fastest growing sports in the world. With this explosion in participation comes the need to know more about how players and coaches can improve their performance and enjoyment of the game. That's the purpose behind *Winning Roller Hockey.*

In these pages you'll find a comprehensive look at roller hockey, from how to select proper equipment to learning advanced team strategies. Whether you're a player or coach, this book gives you an in-depth look at how to excel in this challenging sport. The book is organized in a way that players and coaches can acquire the knowledge and skills they need to advance their game to the next level. Each chapter examines a key dimension of roller hockey and moves from basic ideas and drills to more advanced concepts. This means there is something for everyone throughout the book, regardless of skill level. An abundance of practical practice and game tips combined with a comprehensive set of drills are presented here in an accessible, easy-to-read format. At the end of the book, sample practice plans are provided to demonstrate how to integrate the drills and activities into your practice sessions.

Throughout this book we tried to use language that was gender-inclusive, but the alternatives to some common terms (such as man-to-man) are so awkward that we stayed with traditional usage. It is not our intention to be exclusive. Increasingly large numbers of women are involved in roller hockey, and we wrote this book to improve the play of both males and females.

Whether you have played roller hockey competitively or are about to put on wheels for the first time, *Winning Roller Hockey* has all you'll need to enjoy this exciting game "to the max."

key to drills

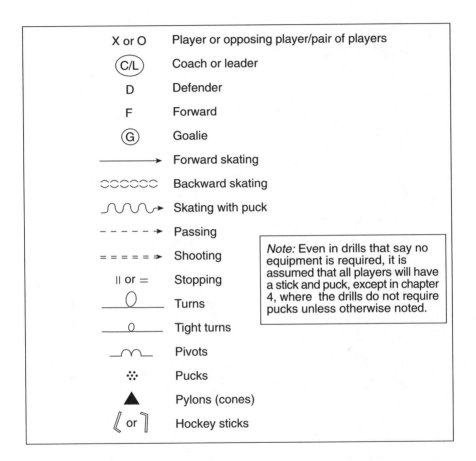

X or O	Player or opposing player/pair of players
(C/L)	Coach or leader
D	Defender
F	Forward
(G)	Goalie
⟶	Forward skating
⟳⟳⟳⟳⟳⟳	Backward skating
∿∿∿→	Skating with puck
- - - - →	Passing
= = = = →	Shooting
‖ or =	Stopping
Turns	Turns
Tight turns	Tight turns
Pivots	Pivots
⋰	Pucks
▲	Pylons (cones)
⟮ or ⟯	Hockey sticks

Note: Even in drills that say no equipment is required, it is assumed that all players will have a stick and puck, except in chapter 4, where the drills do not require pucks unless otherwise noted.

drill finder

The Drill Finder identifies the aspects of roller hockey incorporated into each drill beyond the primary skill area of the chapter in which it appears. The Drill Finder will show you the many different ways you can use each drill. There is no "skating" category in this chart as virtually all of the drills develop skating as a foundational aspect of play.

Drill #	Drill	Puck Control	Passing/Receiving	Shooting	Pressure	Game Related Activity	Goalie Involvement	Conditioning	Fun Activity
1	Snake							●	
2	Three Up and Out							●	
3	The Loop							●	
4	Tight Turn Killer							●	
5	Backward Clear							●	
6	Long Figure 8							●	
7	Lead Dog							●	●
8	Partner Pull							●	●
9	Puck Control Warm-Up	●							●
10	Face the Flag	●							
11	Pylon Madness	●		●					●
12	Circuit	●						●	●
13	Turncoat	●		●					●
14	The Rabbit	●		●	●	●	●	●	
15	Face the Music	●		●				●	●
16	Off the Hip	●		●				●	●
17	Puck Control Shinney	●		●			●	●	●
18	Corner Crunch	●		●	●	●	●	●	●
19	Partner Pass		●						
20	Line Pass		●	●			●		
21	Passing Triangle		●	●			●		
22	Russian Wheel		●	●			●	●	
23	One-Touch Square		●	●			●	●	
24	Three-Pass Kicker		●	●		●	●	●	●
25	Four-on-Two Finish	●	●	●	●	●	●	●	
26	Hoyer 2 by 2	●	●	●	●	●	●	●	
27	Three-on-Three Battle	●	●	●	●	●	●	●	
28	Three-Line Rush	●	●	●	●	●	●	●	
29	Full Rink Rockets	●		●			●	●	
30	Board Pops	●	●	●			●	●	
31	Circle Attack			●			●		
32	Center Pivots	●	●	●			●		
33	Denver Tights		●	●			●		
34	Three Shot Drill		●	●			●		

Drill

Drill #	Drill	Puck Control	Passing/Receiving	Shooting	Pressure	Game Related Activity	Goalie Involvement	Conditioning	Fun Activity
35	Coach's Choice		●	●			●		
36	Red Line Down	●		●	●	●	●	●	
37	Hitch a Ride	●		●	●	●	●	●	
38	Bulldog			●	●	●	●	●	●
39	Horseshoe			●			●		
40	Rapid Fire	●		●			●		
41	Get the Handle	●	●	●			●		
42	Goalie Wide Run	●	●	●			●		
43	Killer's Bump	●	●	●			●		
44	Tip Time		●	●			●		●
45	Screen Door	●		●	●	●	●		
46	Three Shot Fever			●			●		
47	Center Scramble	●	●	●	●	●	●		●
48	Angle Showdown	●		●			●		●
49	One-on-One Full Rink	●		●	●	●	●	●	
50	Two-on-One Attack	●	●	●	●	●	●	●	
51	Option Three-on-Two	●	●	●	●	●	●	●	
52	Cycling	●	●	●	●	●	●		
53	Back Door Feed	●	●	●		●	●		
54	Wide Rim Tip		●	●		●	●		
55	Spinnerama	●	●	●	●	●	●		
56	Second Wave	●	●	●		●	●		
57	Long Bomb	●	●	●		●	●		
58	Space Lob	●	●	●		●	●		
59	The Trailer		●	●			●		
60	Shutdown	●	●			●			
61	Contain to Corner	●	●	●	●	●	●	●	
62	Gap Control	●		●	●	●	●	●	
63	Lock-Up	●		●	●	●	●	●	
64	Static Box	●	●	●	●	●	●		
65	Triangle Plus One	●	●	●	●	●	●		
66	The Diamond	●	●	●	●	●	●		
67	Two-on-Two Low	●	●	●	●	●	●	●	
68	Three-on-Three Low	●	●	●	●	●	●	●	

1

Getting Started

Here's information to help any roller hockey enthusiast prepare for the game. Included in this chapter are keys to success that highlight the concepts that need to be addressed before attempting to play; a section that compares several aspects of roller hockey to ice hockey, noting differences for those switching from ice to pavement; and a checklist with quick facts that help you understand the rules and important concepts for playing the game to the best of your ability.

KEYS TO ROLLER HOCKEY SUCCESS

Whether you're a beginner or an experienced player, learning and becoming more adept at roller hockey is constantly challenging. Beginners must establish a strong foundation for proper skill development, whereas veteran players must continually work to perfect their skills. Here we'll introduce key components of roller hockey and explain how to approach them.

Choose the Proper Equipment for *You*

The most important piece of equipment is your skates. The old adage "you get what you pay for" is probably true when you're selecting your skates. By researching competing products and purchasing high-quality equipment that is right for you given your level of play, you'll significantly increase your chances of improving your roller hockey skills and enjoyment of the game. Read the material on selecting skates on pages 10-12. Similarly, whether you're choosing a helmet, stick, or other equipment, you need a proper fit that feels comfortable and provides maximum protection. Remember that skates and other equipment will influence your learning curve, so take your time and purchase wisely.

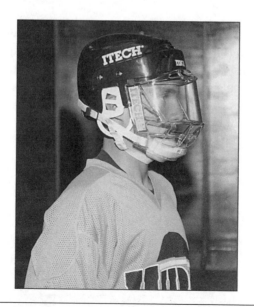

Good face and head protection are a must for safe play.

Skating Is the Foundation of All Roller Hockey Success

Once you've selected the right equipment for you, your next step is to become comfortable with skating. If you don't have proper skating technique, you won't progress very far in roller hockey, and you'll be frustrated. Ice hockey coaches constantly tell their players that to fully enjoy their sport they need to get as much ice time as possible. Similarly, to improve their enjoyment of the game, roller hockey players must get ample time on the pavement. Look for a location where you won't be constantly bumping into people, especially if you're a beginner and can't stop very well. Skating for roller hockey will be described in greater detail in chapter 4—for now, realize that for the rest of your game to improve, you need to spend as much time as you can learning to in-line skate. Without a doubt, skating should be the focus for both beginners *and* pro players!

Protect Yourself Against Injury

Nothing is more frustrating for athletes than being repeatedly injured and unable to play their sports to the maximum. As previously noted, protecting yourself involves choosing the proper equipment. However, protection goes beyond equipment. In chapter 3, we will examine issues that all roller players should consider to enjoy the game at minimal risk. For example, we'll describe a stretching routine to reduce injury. We'll also discuss proper hydration within the context of the roller environment. In your early roller playing development, the last thing you want to do is put yourself at risk.

Get Involved With a Skill Appropriate Group

Most leagues and associations are based on age. While such categorizing helps solve an administrative problem, it does not help many roller hockey hopefuls. Try to get involved with players of similar skill range, regardless of age! Your local recreation association may have a Learn to Roller Skate program, which might be ideal if you're just getting started. If you're a more advanced player, consider joining a roller league in your city. The key is to do your homework and decide where the proper fit is for you. Rome wasn't built in a day, and your roller hockey skills won't magically develop either. Become involved at a level comfortable for you, allowing for both enjoyment and success at the game.

From Ice to Pavement

The jump from ice to pavement may seem a natural one, since the sports share many rules and principles of play. However, the differences between pavement and ice present unique problems to those making the switch.

Skates. On ice, virtually the entire blade surface will be in contact with the ice sheet while gliding. In roller hockey, you'll never have the entire surface of all wheels in contact with the pavement at the same time. Some players who play both sports say that roller skating is actually easier to master than ice skating because roller wheels provide more initial stability than the thin steel blades on ice skates. For now, it's enough to say that players who participate in both sports or who switch from one to the other will have to adjust to the difference in feel, and this can take time.

Playing surface. Ice provides less friction than any roller hockey surface, which means that roller players will not be able to glide as easily or at the same speed as ice hockey players. It also means that roller hockey players must spend more energy than their ice hockey counterparts to achieve the same results. Although other factors will affect energy expenditure, such as skate quality and physical conditioning, players making the switch from ice to pavement should be aware of the differences in glide between the two sports.

Stopping. Ice hockey skaters soon realize that stopping in roller hockey presents a whole new set of challenges. It is very difficult to stop quickly on in-line skates, and the two-foot stop so common in ice hockey is reserved for only the most advanced roller players. Because stopping is so difficult, turning becomes extra important in roller hockey, perhaps more so than on ice, as we'll discuss in chapter 4.

Strategy. If you're switching from ice to roller hockey, consider the strategic differences in the game resulting from the absence of offside calls. In roller hockey a turnover can very quickly lead to goal-scoring opportunities for opponents, so you must rethink your positioning and provide ample support to teammates who have the puck and are under pressure. Otherwise, turnovers will consistently cost your team. A player should resist the urge to move the puck forward by passing to a teammate in favor of controlling it for better strategic advantage. For example, often the puck carrier can delay to allow teammates to set a screen in front of the opponent's net, creating a confusing situation for the goaltender under attack.

Below we provide a reference chart of the major differences between ice hockey and roller hockey. If you're an ice hockey player making the switch to pavement, modify your game according to the factors presented and your transition will be enjoyable and effective.

FROM ICE TO PAVEMENT: A COMPARATIVE CHART

CATEGORY	ICE HOCKEY	ROLLER HOCKEY
Skating	• Easier to achieve full extension of pushing leg, gliding phase will be longer. • Stops such as a two-foot stop or one-foot drag are relatively easy.	• More friction between playing surface and wheels means less glide. • Stopping is much more difficult; emphasis shifts to turning and pivoting.
Passing	• Puck will run or glide more making tape-to-tape passes easier. • Target area for delivering the pass is only slightly ahead of the receiver.	• Friction restricts the glide of the puck. • Passer should pass to *areas* of the rink more often, rather than tape to tape. • Target area is further ahead—you need to lead the receiver.
Shooting	• Players have considerable time to set up and shoot, as the puck glides at virtually the same speed as the player.	• Players must set up and release quickly, as the puck will not glide as well. • Working on one-time release is very important.
Team Play	• Physical play is more common and vital. • Players must be aware of offside rules when approaching blueline. • The line markings (blue/red/blue) affect team strategies, especially to neutral zone and defensive coverages.	• High skill level is a vital component. • No offside, so players head into offensive situations more quickly. • No line markings, so players must support teammates who have the puck and are being pressured.

ROLLER HOCKEY CHECKLIST

Here are some more important points for you to consider when playing roller hockey:

1. Roller hockey requires great patience and confidence when controlling the puck. Players must work at mastering puck control.
2. Because roller hockey is largely a game of puck control and possession, giving the puck up, often referred to as "dump and chase," is not a preferred strategy.
3. Master your skating skills. Focus particularly on stopping and quick-turning techniques.
4. One-time shooting is important to master. Players should be able to shoot a puck directly from a pass without having to stop it first, which requires a single, smooth motion at the point of release. Skillful one-time shooting takes considerable time and practice to achieve.
5. Roller hockey offense is similar to basketball offense. Like the basketball, the puck is brought into the offensive zone, held, and then passed until the team has a good shot on net.
6. Roller hockey lends itself to many set plays, including picks or screens as in basketball, and fast breaks as in soccer.

Roller Hockey Quick Facts*

- Four skaters and one goalie per side during play
- 14 players per team
- No offsides, two-line passes, or icing
- Two periods of play, each 20 minutes in length
- 5 minutes of rest between periods
- No body checking, limited physical contact
- 2-minute minor penalties
- Power plays can be four-vs-three, four-vs-two, or three-vs-two
- Minimum number of skaters during play is two per team

- Playing surface may be cement, asphalt, or another form of sport court
- Puck is 3 inches in diameter and 3.5 ounces
- Net dimensions—Professional: 6 feet by 4 feet; International: 5 feet by 41 inches

*Check with your league to see if any of this information is different in your area.

IN SUMMARY

Follow these basic guidelines to make roller hockey a safe and enjoyable pastime:

1. **Buy equipment appropriate for your own needs.**
2. **Get as much asphalt or pavement time as possible.** Practice might not make perfect, but working on your skating is sure to improve your overall game.
3. **Protect yourself against injury.** Don't overextend yourself; be sure to warm up and stretch before playing.
4. **Associate with a skill appropriate group.** Don't try to play with high-level players before you're ready.
5. **If you're making the switch from ice to pavement, consider the key differences described in this chapter.**

2

Equipment

Ever since mass production of in-line skates began in the 1980s, roller hockey has steadily become one of the fastest growing sports in the world. Not surprisingly, a roller hockey player's choices in equipment have also increased dramatically. With all that's out there now, before you purchase any equipment, you need to know what's available and what suits you best. The equipment you choose when beginning in roller hockey can significantly affect how fast and well you develop your skills.

Because skates are central to your success as a roller hockey player, we'll first discuss proper skate selection and provide an equipment chart that summarizes what you will need to consider before buying your equipment.

SKATES

Your skates are the most important single purchase you'll make. The many models and types companies offer all have a place in blading, whether designed for the casual participant or the professional player. The key for anyone buying skates is to buy the right skate for the intended application. If you plan to become involved in a league with a heavy practice and game schedule, you'll want to pick a skate that can withstand wear and tear. On the other hand (or in this case, foot!), it would not be very smart to invest in top-of-the-line skates when your main purpose is to engage in a Sunday skate every other week.

Let's take a look now at the three main components of in-line skates and what you should consider before making a purchase.

THE FRAME

The frame is the part of the skate that holds the wheels in line; most frames are designed to hold four wheels. Frames are made of many different materials. Some are 100% plastic, whereas others are nylon and/or metal, either alone or in some combination with plastic. A general rule of thumb is the stiffer the frame, the better the durability. Some of the most durable frames are made of aluminum, the material of choice among many pro players.

Make sure the frame is well attached to the boot. If you give a quick tug on the frame, you should not feel any looseness between it and the boot. Also look for gaps along the frame/boot line, as these could lead to trouble down the road.

THE BOOT

There are two main types of boots on the market: stitched and injection molded. The stitched boot resembles an ice hockey skate converted for in-line skating (many major ice hockey skate manufacturers are now doing exactly that). The injection molded boot is plastic, unstitched, and looks like a downhill skiing boot.

Your choice of type of boot should depend on what feels right to you and what your intentions are. If you intend to play only occasionally, don't buy top-of-the-line skates unless you have money to burn. Conversely, if you're active in the game, you'll want a boot that will form to your feet and last for years, thus justifying the expense for state-of-the-art boots.

If you're a serious player, you might consider memory foam inserts, which mold precisely to your foot. Or, if you have weak ankles, you might want the added support you get from a high-cuff boot. These features add expense, but many consider them worth it.

When purchasing skates, remember that the boot *must fit properly* for you to maximize your skill development. Many parents purchase skates one or two sizes too big for their children so they'll grow into them. But this apparent economy can put a young player at a great disadvantage. If your foot is loose in the boot, your balance can be thrown off, which will affect your ability to play and increase the potential for injury. Not many people would wear running shoes two sizes too big to run a marathon. It would be just as foolish to try to play roller hockey in boots that don't fit.

Boots that fit properly help you play to your maximum ability and reduce your chances of injury.

THE WHEELS

You need to consider wheel size, bearings, and composition when considering what skates to purchase.

- Wheels come in various sizes, with a 70-mm wheel being the most suitable for newer players. The bigger the wheel, the more friction created, so lean toward small wheels until you become a skilled player.

- Look for skates with superior bearings, as these will make skating easier. The ABEC Rating System is a good reference to check when determining the quality of bearings. This system uses a 1-3-5 rating scale where the higher the number, the faster and smoother the bearing will be. There are many companies that supply bearings for wheels, so it's best to check with your supplier to ensure that the bearings in your skates are of highest quality. In general, the cheaper the skate, the cheaper the bearings.

- Depending on what they're made of, some wheels will be more effective than others on specific surfaces. At elite levels of play, roller skates can be customized taking surface conditions and needs into account. For example, the outside two wheels might be made of one grade material, while the inside two wheels could be made of another. If you know in advance what surface you'll be skating on, tell the salesperson and try to match the wheels accordingly.

OTHER EQUIPMENT

Use the equipment checklist on page 15 as a quick reference when purchasing required roller hockey equipment. Do your research on all of these products to ensure that you'll get the best return on your investment. There are several magazines and publications that provide important information about equipment. For example, *The In-Line Retailer and Industry News* (Boulder, CO) has in-depth reports on what's new for in-line and roller hockey equipment. *USA Hockey In-Line* (Colorado Springs) and *Roller Hockey* magazine (Los Angeles) are other useful resources. Helmets purchased should be certified as safe by either the Canadian Standards Association (CSA) in Canada or Hockey Equipment Certification Council (HECC) in the United

States. These agencies test to ensure that you will receive the best protection possible. Of course, another important source for information is players who have tried different types of equipment and can offer practical insights into what works, what stands up over time, and what brand names or types of equipment to avoid. Check with your local roller hockey suppliers to see what products are available to you.

Once you get involved with the game, you'll find that a lot of players do not use all the safety equipment we recommend. They think it's unnecessary since the rules of most roller hockey leagues forbid the kind of body contact you see in ice hockey. Some players do not use their helmets because they feel cumbersome or don't wear shoulder pads because they feel too hot. These types of attitudes can lead to serious injury. Roller hockey is a very fast game played on a hard surface, and accidents happen. Even in practice situations, you should always wear a helmet with a full face shield or mask, while including some form of shoulder protection. Better to be a little hot than end up with a broken shoulder and out of the game for months.

After reading these warnings, you may be surprised that not all the safety equipment is worn in some of the photos in this book. Don't conclude from this that we have a casual attitude toward protective equipment. Sometimes we deliberately left off the equipment to show clearly the correct position of the arms or legs; and sometimes we were taking pictures in game or practice situations that weren't led by us, so it wasn't up to us to dictate equipment use to the players. Just remember: Imitate the technique, not the lack of safety equipment!

ROLLER HOCKEY EQUIPMENT CHECKLIST

Here's a quick checklist to use when purchasing roller hockey equipment. When buying protective gear, remember to look for a HECC or CSA certified product to ensure quality. The selection of hockey sticks in the market has grown considerably, and players must decide what is the best fit for them. Stick length and weight is a personal choice—there's no formula to determine how long or heavy your stick should be. Various stick manufacturers produce equipment with different degrees of blade curvature. A player's skill level will affect how much blade curve to use; generally, the more curve you have, the more skill you'll need to control the puck. As environmental conditions vary greatly, simple questions like, "What do I wear under my protective gear?" will need to be addressed depending on your local situation. Any undergarments should be as lightweight as possible and made of fabrics that allow perspiration to evaporate, which will help you keep cool during play. You may find that your needs call for specific types of equipment, so check with players, coaches, league officials, or retailers before investing in the equipment listed in the chart.

EQUIPMENT CONSIDERATIONS CHART

EQUIPMENT TYPE	CONSIDERATIONS	COMMENTS
Protective Gear	• Helmet • Gloves • Pants • Shoulder pads • Elbow pads • Shin pads • Neck guard • Mouth guard	• Purchase only CSA or HECC certified helmets. • Buy well-ventilated gloves, especially for use in facilities that don't have air conditioning. • Depending on league rules, you may need to use a mouth guard and protective face shield.
Sticks	• Different compositions • Length • Weight • Blade curvature	• Choose from wood, graphite, aluminum, or other composite materials—cost will affect your choice! • Comfort is key in stick selection.
Skates	• Frame • Boot • Wheels	• Make sure to buy skates that fit properly. • Keep frames and wheels clean, free from dirt. • Rotate wheels often.
Other Equipment	• Undergarments (includes protective cup) • Equipment bag • Uniforms (jerseys) • Water bottle (fluids) • First-aid materials	• If involved in a formal league, much, if not all of these materials will be provided. When purchasing for personal use, determine needs first, then purchase accordingly.

Note: If you need to purchase pucks, we recommend "slider" roller pucks for league play as opposed to the bearing-type pucks also available. Sliders tend to lie flatter on roller surfaces while bearing types are more appropriate for street use.

3

Conditioning and Safety

You need to be ready for the stress that regular roller hockey places on your body. If you're a once-a-week player, you probably won't need to worry about elite-level conditioning, though you will want to read this chapter for its information on safety. If you're thinking about becoming serious in the sport, you need to learn what kind of physical preparation you need before you begin playing regularly. You should also review safety concerns so you can enjoy the maximum benefits of the sport with a minimum of risk.

CONDITIONING KEYS

Roller hockey is a physically taxing game that makes demands of all the energy systems and major muscle groups of the body. If you want to play high-level roller hockey, you need a high level of overall fitness. Trying to play hard before you're ready is just asking for an injury. Prepare yourself for roller hockey action by following the keys below.

Prepare Yourself for the Rigors of Roller Hockey by Engaging in Preseason Training

There are many programs, books, and videos available to provide players with sound generic training guidelines to improve fitness levels in preparation for roller hockey action. Check with your roller hockey supplier for current information—and don't wait for the season to begin before you address your fitness level for the sport. In any preparatory conditioning, it's wise to consider some basic principles to maximize your training efforts:

• Roller hockey is primarily an *anaerobic* activity supported by an aerobic foundation. This means roller players should emphasize sprint activities, either through running or bicycle work, that simulates the explosive nature of roller hockey.

• When conditioning, focus on lower body power and strength. Consider activities such as vertical jumping and other plyometric exercises to improve the lower body, as this will greatly affect your skating efficiency.

• Develop all of the abdominal muscle groups—another key area for roller players. Roller hockey is a game of constant change of direction through quick pivots and turns. It's important that the various layers of abdominal muscles be developed to avoid what can be very painful and long-term injuries.

Do a Warm-Up Routine Before Each Training Session or Game

This routine could include a light jog to warm up the legs and upper body, followed by a simple stretching routine as described in the following pages. It's important to wait until enough blood enters the major muscle areas before beginning any significant stretching of these groups. Only after you start to feel warm, perhaps after you have begun to sweat, should you attempt to loosen the larger muscle groups such as in the leg and trunk area. This will reduce the number of strains or pulls that can result from muscle tissue being exercised or stretched before being properly prepared. Many teams do these warm-up activities as a unit before a practice or game. However, if your group does not warm up as a team, do it on your own time.

Spend Time After Training or Competing to Cool Down Your Body and Mind

As your muscles are heated from competition and thus more easily manipulated, immediately after a practice or competition may be the best time to do stretching exercises. This is when flexibility can truly be affected, and flexibility is one area of fitness that many players fail to recognize as important. The physical demands of roller hockey make flexibility a key component of fitness, and becoming increasingly flexible helps ensure your safety as a roller hockey player. A cool-down period also allows you to reflect on your recently completed training session or game. Use this time to self-assess with the goal of improving future workouts.

When Training, Work With a Partner or in a Group

The preparatory phase of conditioning for any athlete can be a burden, causing many players to skip a session or to work at an unacceptable level. Having a partner or group of people involved in your conditioning makes the activity more fun; you'll also begin to push each other in your workout routines, maximizing the training effect.

Make Training a Part of Your Lifestyle

Many players complain that conditioning or training workouts are boring, so their results are unsatisfying. Try to include activities that you enjoy in your training program so that you look forward to your sessions. Any serious roller player must be committed to a lifestyle with conditioning as a priority of the daily routine.

As previously noted, players should check out the latest training protocols and, as appropriate, incorporate aspects of these programs into their personal training regimen. Roller hockey is still a relatively new sport worldwide, so extensive sport-specific programs are not available. If you can't find such programs, check out ice hockey references. Many of the same muscle groups and actions are used on both pavement and ice, so using ice hockey training techniques is a safe and useful way of beginning your roller hockey fitness program. Check the section called Roller Hockey Stretches for some quick and easy stretching exercises designed to prepare muscle groups before and after a workout.

SAFETY

As in any sporting activity, roller hockey players and coaches must be aware of safety in both preparation and play. Inexperienced players need to be especially careful in this regard. As we mentioned in the previous chapter, you need protective gear to help ensure that your playing time will be safe and injury-free. After all, no one wants to see his or her name on an injury reserved list after only one attempt at this exciting sport. To get started on a positive note, remember the key aspects of safety listed below.

Notice the Surface

• When heading out for skating activities on city streets, watch for uneven surfaces or potholes. Do some scouting to find locations with smooth surfaces. It's difficult to master skating when you must constantly watch for difficult stretches of road or pavement.

• Avoid any water, sand, oil, or pebbles. These obstacles detract from learning proper skating technique and cause unnecessary wear and tear on your skates, specifically the wheels. In addition, something as small as a discarded piece of gum on a playing surface may lead to falls. Check your skating surface carefully to avoid these problems.

• In games or game-like practices, make sure to dispense drinks to players in a way that doesn't affect the playing surface. Players need to continuously drink water or some other fluid to replenish the body during roller hockey activities. But liquid of any type on the playing surface is potentially dangerous and should be avoided. Keep water bottles where liquid will not leak onto the floor of the bench area, from which it could be tracked by players onto the playing surface. Placing towels on the floor of the bench area is an effective way to absorb any excess liquids and will be helpful in both cleaning and drying wheels before each shift during a practice or game. This is especially useful during hot and humid playing conditions. Also, plastic pails (for liquid disposal) should be made available near the bench area for players who wish to rinse out their mouths during rest periods. Again, this is a preventive measure that will keep liquids away from the playing surface.

Maintain Your Equipment Properly

• Rotate your wheels often to distribute wear and tear evenly. This will extend the life of your wheels and ensure that you get maximum performance and efficiency out of your efforts.

• Make sure all equipment is intact and in good working order. Check that your helmet does not have any cracks or worn straps. Be sure that all your gear can do what it is designed to do. If a shin guard needs a new strap or a glove requires repalming, get it done quickly so that you can be sure that you're safe while playing.

Practice Stopping Before Heading Out Into Uncharted Waters

You need confidence in your ability to change direction or stop in a hurry, especially on the open road. These skills will serve you well in game situations, so take the time under controlled conditions to practice stopping and quick turns.

Consider the Safety of Your Opponents

For example, players should always keep their sticks under control to avoid hitting others. In leagues where contact is allowed, the safety of all concerned must be a principle of play, meaning that any contact where opponents cannot defend themselves should be strictly forbidden. Everyone involved in roller hockey competition deserves the opportunity to participate with a low risk of injury. Players must be held accountable for any intentional action that may cause injury to others.

Be Aware of Heat-Related Problems

As a final safety note, remember that roller hockey venues are often extremely hot and humid, making players susceptible to heat-related problems. Trainers, coaches, and players should all become familiar with the symptoms associated with heat exhaustion. For example, be alert to any player who complains of extreme headaches or talks of being "light headed." Players who are nauseous or feel the need to vomit may also be on the verge of suffering heat exhaustion. Any player who becomes disoriented, loses coordination, or faints during a game could also be indicating some sort of heat-related problem. As a preventive measure we recommend that teams have cold towels near the bench area, available for players to use as a cool-down mechanism. If possible, ice should be made available as well.

If these simple safety practices are observed, roller hockey will continue to grow as a popular activity among all age groups.

ROLLER HOCKEY STRETCHES

The following stretching activities can be done in full hockey gear either before or after a practice or game. When attempting these stretches, remember,

1. Never stretch past the point of pain. If you feel uncomfortable, ease off. Otherwise, you may be producing microtears in your muscles, which will make you less, not more, flexible.

2. Stretch like a cat. This is a good visual that reminds us to stretch slowly and fully. You should be in no hurry when stretching.

3. Avoid excessive strain on joints, especially the knee. Bend slightly at the knee joint when doing weight bearing leg stretches to reduce pressure on surrounding capsule structures.

4. Do not bounce during stretching.

5. Be careful if you hold weights to add resistance.

6. Concentrate on proper breathing as a means of relaxation during stretching.

7. Stretch the bigger muscle groups near the end of your stretching routine.

There are many stretches to choose from in designing a routine. The following 10 stretches will work all the muscles you'll use in roller hockey, so if you enjoy the constancy of a standard stretching routine that becomes almost automatic, you need look no farther than this list. If you want to vary your routine, you can get other stretches from many fine resources, including *Sport Stretch* by Michael J. Alter (1990). The choice is yours.

You can do most of these stretches in your shoes, shirt, and shorts, or you can wear your roller hockey equipment for a pregame routine.

SHOULDER CIRCLES

Procedure

1. Extend each arm out to the side.
2. Start circling the arms, first small and then gradually larger.
3. Circle the arms clockwise and then counterclockwise.

Notes

- The shoulder region is an important area for roller players and warming these muscles is vital.
- Before a game, players may use the hockey stick in a lassoing motion to circle the arms.
- If a partner is available, loosening of the shoulder girdle can easily be achieved by having the partner stand behind, gently pulling back on the arms as they are circled.
- Resistance may also be added by placing the hands against a wall and pressing lightly while making circles.

LEAN-TO

Procedure

1. Stand with feet flat on the surface about shoulder-width apart.
2. Reach behind the head with one arm and grab the triceps area of the opposite arm.
3. Lean in the direction of the grabbed arm.
4. Hold stretch 5 to 10 seconds to maximize the effect.

Notes

- This stretch pulls the triceps muscles and muscle groups in the upper trunk area.
- In pregame routines, players can hold the hockey stick across their shoulders and lean side to side.

ALL FOURS

Procedure

1. Get on all fours with hands flat on the surface.
2. Keeping the hands stationary, slowly move the body backward until the buttocks touch the legs.
3. Hold stretch for 10 seconds.

Notes

- This stretch will work the shoulder, low back, and hamstring muscle groups.
- Keep the feet inverted, with soles facing up, and slowly lower your buttocks toward your legs.
- The lower back is a common area of injury for hockey players, and this stretch will help loosen that region of the body.

FLAT OUT

Procedure

1. Lie on your back on a flat surface.
2. Extend arms overhead, palms facing up.
3. Stretch arms and legs in opposite directions, pointing the fingers and toes.
4. Hold stretch for 5 seconds and then repeat two more times.

Notes

- A simple yet effective stretch for relaxing a variety of muscle groups, especially before competition.
- For maximum effect, stretch the toes and fingers.

LEG LOCK

Procedure

1. Lie on your back with hands behind your head.
2. Keeping your shoulders in contact with the surface, roll over to one hip.
3. Bring the leg of the hip you rolled onto over the top of the other leg.
4. Hold stretch for 10 seconds on each side.

Notes

- This is a key stretch for the sacroiliac and low back area, and players should feel the stretch throughout these regions.
- Change the position of the bottom leg to alter the stretch angle.
- Try to keep shoulders flat to the surface.
- Repeat this stretch often, both in training and during pregame warm-up.

FLYING V

Procedure

1. Sit with legs spread apart in a V-formation.

2. Place hands flat on the surface in front of you and slowly bend forward at the hip, keeping your head up and looking forward.

3. Hold stretch for 10 seconds. (Initially you won't be able to hold this position very long.)

Notes

- This is a very taxing stretch.
- You should feel a pulling sensation in the groin area, lower back, and buttocks.
- Don't bounce during this stretch.
- Build up to greater upper body lean.
- Bend slightly at the knee to minimize discomfort.

INSIDE OUT

Procedure

1. Sit with arms behind your body and palms face down.
2. Bend your knees and draw your feet in the same direction.
3. Lean back slightly on supporting arms and feel the tension in the front of the legs increase.
4. Hold stretch for 10 seconds on each side.

Notes

- This is a variation of the traditional hurdler's stretch.
- This is an important stretch for roller players, as it loosens the quadriceps muscles along the front portion of the legs. These big muscle groups are important in skating.

WISHBONE

Procedure

1. Sit with the soles of your feet together.

2. Bring your feet in as close as you comfortably can toward your body.

3. Grab your feet with your hands and, with head down, slightly bend forward at the waist.

4. Hold this stretch for 10 seconds.

Notes

- This stretch affects flexibility over the long term, something many roller players lack.

- By drawing the feet closer to the body, you'll feel increased tension and pull in both the groin area and hamstring muscles in the back of the legs.

- By leaning forward more, you'll maximize the stretch.

SCISSORS

Procedure

1. Stand in a lunge position.
2. Bend front knee to approximately 90 degrees.
3. Looking forward, slowly lower your body down, placing hands and back knee on the floor for stability.
4. Hold stretch for 10 seconds on each leg.

Notes

- An excellent stretch for several major muscle groups in the legs, especially the hamstrings and calf muscles.
- This stretch loosens the Achilles tendon, an often overlooked yet vital body part for effective skating.

I SPY

Procedure

1. Stand a little more than an arm's length away from a wall.
2. Put one leg forward, bend at the knee, and place hands on wall.
3. Rest your head on your hands.
4. Keeping your back leg in a straight line, lean forward at the hips.
5. Hold stretch for 10 seconds on each leg.

Notes

- A simple stretch you can do against a wall or along the boards/ glass before a game.
- This activity is designed especially for the Achilles tendon and calf muscles.

4

Skating

Whether on pavement, asphalt, or ice, skating is the fundamental skill that all hockey players should constantly practice to improve. In roller hockey, players must recognize the limitations that both skates and surfaces present and work on technique to minimize their impact.

If you have any experience at all as a roller player, you know that stopping quickly is very difficult in this sport. This being the case, turning—especially quick turns and pivots—is a vital part of blading. To reinforce the skills you'll need, most if not all practice sessions should include skating drills that focus on turning and pivoting.

Players also need to establish proper skating mechanics through full knee and ankle extension. This will allow them to achieve maximum glide with a minimum of effort, saving their energy stores for later in the game. Proper technique takes years of practice to perfect, and drilling activities and patterns should incorporate as many skating variations as possible. Pivots, turns, straight-line skating, backward skating, and crossovers should all be included in skating drills. Whether they're beginners or professionals, players must spend time working on their skating as the foundation for all other aspects of play. Without sound skating mechanics, other areas such as shooting, passing, and checking all suffer. Players who attend to the fundamentals of skating will find their playing and practice time becoming increasingly simple, automatic, and enjoyable.

What follows are key teaching areas to reinforce through skating drills. It is often appropriate, especially with newer players, to practice specific skills in isolation, emphasizing particular aspects of skating.

Good knee-bend and ankle extension are essential for efficient skating.

Lower Body

• To maximize efficiency of movement, players need to develop sound knee-bend. Try to achieve a 90-degree bend in the front (support) leg.

• When striding, extend the back (pushing) leg to a straight line position. This will ensure that you get the greatest return on the energy you spend.

• Do not lift your heels excessively high off the playing surface, especially when recovering under the body. Doing so wastes time, power, and energy.

• Keep body weight evenly distributed over both legs and avoid excessive shifting from side to side. Such shifting can result in losing balance and make turning or pivoting tough to control.

Upper Body

• Be mindful of proper upper body alignment in relation to the lower body. The ideal position will find the chin, knee, and toe in a straight line from top to bottom.

• Eyes should be looking out, not down, with shoulders square to the direction you're heading.

• Arms should not cross the center line of the body and should be moving in a forward/backward line as opposed to side to side. Excessive arm movements across the body detract from forward speed.

Stopping

• Stopping is difficult in roller hockey. Many players find it easier to turn or pivot quickly rather than trying to stop.

• Some roller players use a back leg drag technique to slow down and lead into a change of direction. Do this by allowing your back skate to dig into the surface, using the sides of the wheels. Once speed is reduced, you can begin a pivot or tight turn.

• The two-foot stop, as seen in ice hockey, is very difficult on roller surfaces and takes considerable skill and practice. Attempt this maneuver only when you have become proficient at skating.

Turns and Pivots

• These two extremely important maneuvers are used in many applications of roller hockey.

• Execute glide turns by placing skates in a heel-to-toe alignment while turning your shoulders in the direction you wish to travel, allowing momentum to propel you in that direction. Your feet remain static during a glide turn.

• Do crossover turns by bringing one leg (skate) over the other while positioning the skates and body in the intended direction. If executed properly, many skaters can actually accelerate out of a crossover turn rather than lose speed.

• Accomplish pivoting by turning the toe of a skate in the direction you wish to travel, followed by pushing off with the other skate to propel you toward your desired destination. A pivot can be used to move from one side of play to another, or from moving forward to backward and vice versa.

As you practice the skating techniques detailed in this chapter, you will find your skating style becoming more fluid and efficient. However, mastering the skills associated with skating is difficult, so don't get frustrated if you don't see the results you want immediately. Consider these key skating tips while practicing:

Practice in Both Directions

If you're like most skaters, you have a "dominant" leg, meaning you move better in one direction than the other, so you must work to develop your weak side. Roller hockey will not allow you to skate in only one direction, so to take your game to the next level, you must be able to skate strongly to either the left or right.

Learn to Conserve Energy

Get the greatest bang for your skating buck by extending fully with each skating stroke—not only at the knee joint, but also at the ankle. Focus on this idea while practicing. Change won't just happen by itself! Once you're able to fully extend your legs you'll keep more fuel in your energy tank for later in the contest, when it could be vital.

Keep Your Knees Bent

If you remember only one thing from this chapter it should be to keep your knees bent as close to 90 degrees as possible. This is crucial because most of the power generated for skating originates in the big muscle groups of the lower body. By bending your knees to stay lower to the playing surface, you'll activate these big muscles to perform at their explosive best. In addition, by staying low, you'll be more likely to stay upright during the inevitable collisions during games, meaning you spend more time skating and less time picking yourself up! Increasing knee-bend by only a few degrees can dramatically influence your skating style, stability, and efficiency.

Included in this chapter are specific skating drills that provide the foundation players need to develop. If used as they're described, the drills will reinforce proper mechanics through repetition. You can also modify the drills to create more difficult skating patterns and conditions by applying the suggestions listed under Drill Progression(s).

1 SNAKE

Purpose

To work on proper skating technique practicing the three-stride principle

Equipment

None

Time

3 to 5 minutes

Procedure

1. Players form a single line and skate around the rink three strides in one direction followed by three strides in the other direction, in a snake-like motion.
2. Sets should be done skating both forward and backward.

Key Points

- Keep both feet and hands moving at the same time.
- Do not glide in the corners—keep legs moving at all times.

Drill Progressions

- Players work in pairs and shadow their partner.
- Have a trailing partner harass the lead skater with the stick to try to break his or her stride.
- Skate forward one length of the rink and backward the other.
- Handle a puck throughout the drill.

SNAKE

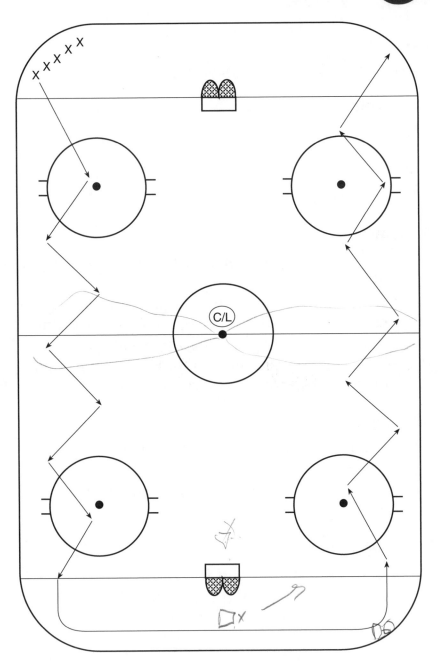

2 THREE UP AND OUT

Purpose

To practice explosive skating using a crossover step

Equipment

None

Time

3 to 5 minutes

Procedure

1. At the whistle, players come out from one corner in groups of three.

2. As the group approaches the mid-rink area, they cross over their legs and cut toward the opposite side of the rink.

3. Once they reach the other side of the rink, players repeat the procedure of crossing over the legs, then head straight into the corner, where all players regroup.

Key Points

- To ensure many repetitions, blow the whistle every 3 seconds.

- Players keep legs moving constantly and attempt to explode forward.

Drill Progressions

- Execute the drill with a puck.

- Use one puck for each group of three and incorporate passing and crossover techniques.

THREE UP AND OUT 2

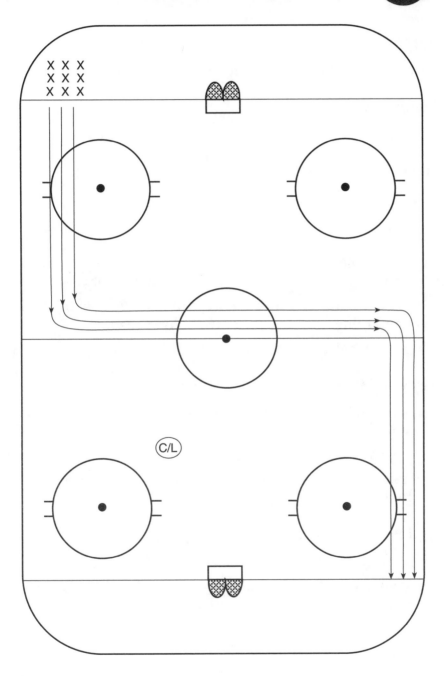

3 THE LOOP

Purpose

To practice quick feet and develop quickness during turns

Equipment

None

Time

3 to 5 minutes

Procedure

1. Assemble players in groups at one end of the rink in four or five lines, depending on the number of players.
2. At the whistle, the first player in each line skates to the center line, then makes a turn at top speed.
3. Player finishes at the other end of the rink.

Key Points

- After the first player begins the turn, the next player in line starts.
- Feet should keep moving throughout the turn.
- Use as small a circle as possible before releasing up the rink to the other end.

Drill Progressions

- Players control a puck.
- Two lines work together, passing one puck between them as they go into and out of their turn.

THE LOOP 3

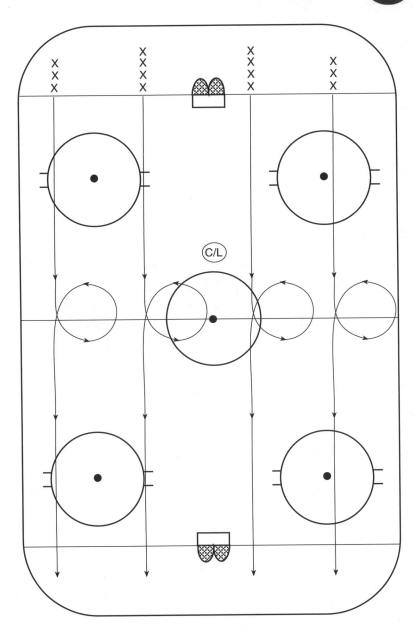

4 TIGHT TURN KILLER

Purpose

To develop tight turn skills using a gliding motion

Equipment

Pylons

Time

4 to 6 minutes

Procedure

1. At one end of the rink players form three, four, or five lines (depending on the number of players).
2. At the whistle the first player skates forward to the pylon and glides 360 degrees while keeping the skates static.
3. Players complete the drill by gliding around each pylon in the lane, finishing at the other end of the rink.

Key Points

- To work on turning skills in both directions, players alternate gliding to the right for one pylon and to the left for the next.
- After a player turns at the first pylon, the next player in line begins.

Drill Progressions

- Increase the number of pylons to force more glide turns.
- Players control a puck during all turns.

TIGHT TURN KILLER

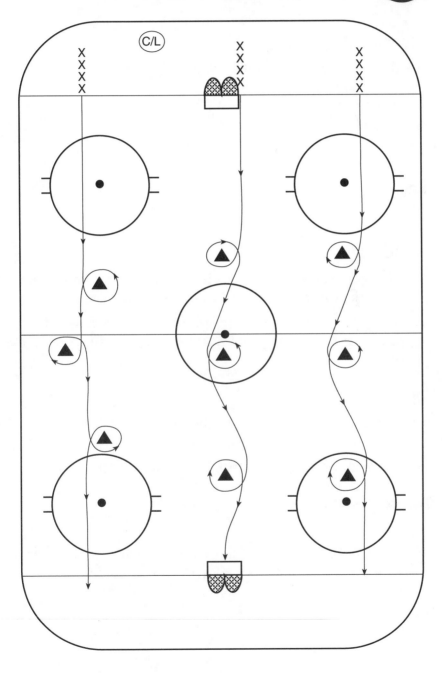

5 BACKWARD CLEAR

Purpose

To develop superior skills in pivoting from backward to forward skating

Equipment

None

Time

2 to 3 minutes

Procedure

1. Allowing each other enough space, players skate around the rink surface backward in the same direction.

2. At the whistle, all players pivot to forward skating for three strides, then pivot backward and continue until the next whistle.

Key Points

- At the whistle players move their feet as quickly as they can until the sequence is completed.

- Everyone should be skating backward when finished.

Drill Progressions

- Add a puck for each player.

- Do a double sequence each whistle (three up, three back, three up, and finish backward).

BACKWARD CLEAR

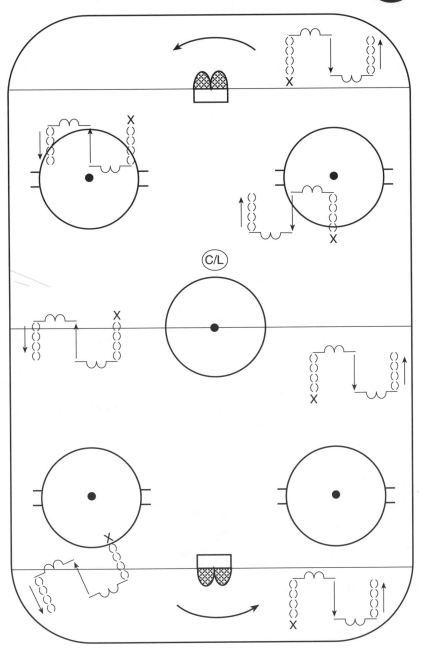

6 LONG FIGURE 8

Purpose

To develop maximum extension (long strides) during full out skating

Equipment

None

Time

4 to 6 minutes

Procedure

1. Players form four equal groups, one group in each corner of the rink.
2. At the whistle, two groups from the same end begin a figure 8 loop, moving in opposite directions across the rink surface.
3. At the next whistle, two players from the other two groups begin their figure 8s.
4. Drill continues at each succeeding whistle, players rotating ends.

Key Points

- Players focus on developing long strides with full knee extension.
- Coaches focus on player technique as opposed to speed.

Drill Progressions

- Try the drill backward (tell players to check over their shoulders to avoid collisions).
- Work in pairs and push each other to increase the pace of the drill.

LONG FIGURE 8 6

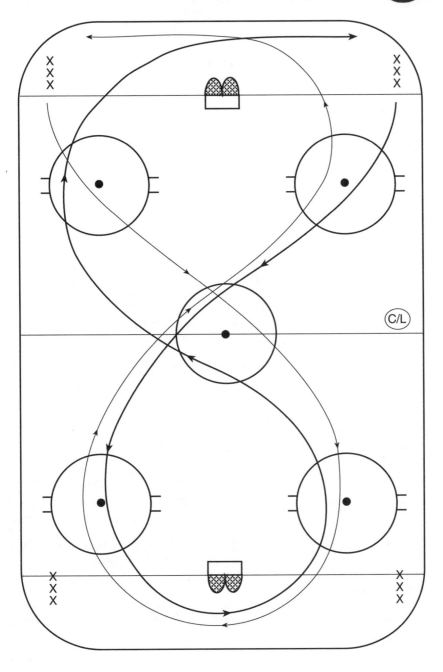

7 LEAD DOG

Purpose

To create an overspeed situation where players extend themselves competitively

Equipment

None

Time

3 to 5 minutes (about 30 seconds per round)

Procedure

1. Divide players into two teams; one team stretches in the center circle while the other skates around the outside of the rink.
2. The front player (the lead dog) has a 10-foot lead to begin (rotate this position).
3. At the whistle, the lead dog sprints as hard as he or she can for two laps to keep from being caught by anyone on the team.
4. At the next whistle, the first team heads to the center for stretching while the other team skates.

Key Points

- Players are in an all-out sprint, so they'll need to rest to achieve maximum results. The necessary rest is provided while the group stretches in the center circle.
- If the lead dog is caught by someone in the group, he or she must serve as lead dog for the next chase as well.

Drill Progressions

- Add pylons around the outside of the rink to form a slalom or obstacle course.
- Give the lead dog a puck.
- Reduce the initial lead from 10 feet to 5 feet.

LEAD DOG

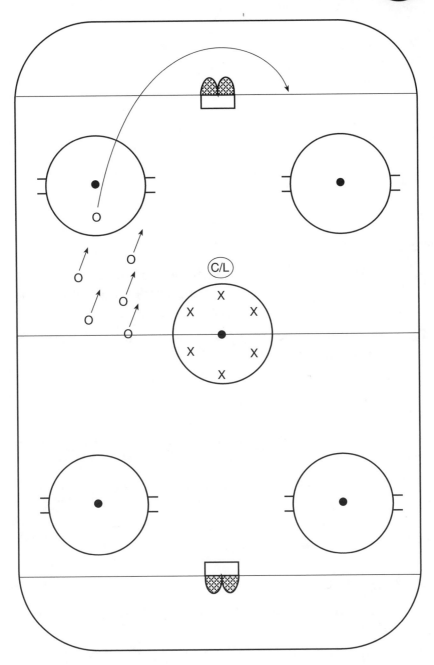

8 PARTNER PULL

Purpose

To develop strength in skating muscle groups while having some fun!

Equipment

Two hockey sticks per pair

Time

3 minutes (30 seconds per set)

Procedure

1. In pairs, one player holds the blade of a hockey stick in each hand while the other stands directly behind holding the shaft of both sticks, one in each hand.
2. At the whistle, the front player pulls the other around the rink until the next whistle.
3. Switch positions after each 30-second pull.

Key Points

- Player who is pulling keeps the knees bent and works on full extension.
- The puller should concentrate on keeping the chest out and eyes looking in the direction the player is moving (i.e., not looking down).
- Player being pulled offers no resistance initially.

Drill Progressions

- Player being pulled digs in skates to make the puller work harder.
- Try the activity with the puller skating backward.

PARTNER PULL

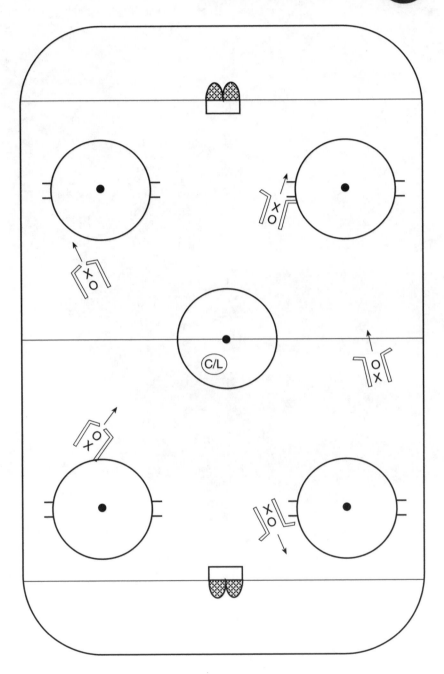

5

Controlling
the Puck

Roller hockey is a modern sport that emphasizes high skill and precision as opposed to mere brute strength. Coaches continually seek out players who demonstrate the ability to control the flow of the game, in part by maintaining possession of the puck. The purpose of this chapter is to highlight some important considerations for players in the development of essential puck control skills. By improving puck control fundamentals, players not only increase their enjoyment of the game but also improve their opportunities for advancement to more elite levels of play.

Let's begin with some fundamentals of practicing puck control as a means of establishing a solid foundation for skill advancement.

1. To avoid losing the puck in the skates, keep your hands and arms away from the body (hips), especially at high speed.

2. For maximum puck control, keep the puck between the center point of the stick blade and the heel (see photo below). Keeping the puck too far up on the blade toward the toe will cause the puck to bounce.

3. Hold the stick with your fingers, not your palm. Fingers are the contact point between the stick and the puck; developing "feel" means that you control the puck through the fine motor control of your fingers (see photo on next page).

4. Work on puck control so that you're looking out, not down, as the feel becomes automatic. This will eventually allow you to make plays you would otherwise not be capable of because your attention is on the puck rather than the game (this takes time, so be patient!).

5. If you have played ice hockey, be aware of the differences between ice and roller surfaces.

Position the puck properly on the stick for maximum puck control.

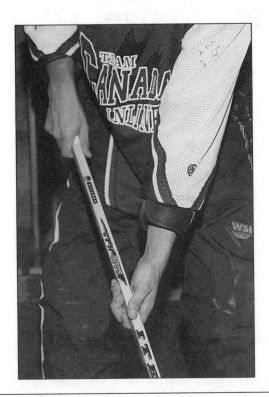

Be sure to control the stick with your fingertips for maximum "feel" of the puck.

Roller hockey players deal with puck control challenges that ice hockey players do not face. For example, roller hockey players have to learn to "cup" the puck by manipulating the angle of the stick blade (see photo on page 58). For players who have spent considerable time playing street hockey, this point is self-evident. By cupping the blade of the stick, players can keep the puck from bouncing on an uneven playing surface. Cupping keeps the puck flat on the surface, enhancing puck control. Also, roller pucks do not roll or slide as easily as pucks do on ice. Players need to push the puck ahead even more than their ice hockey cousins and be stronger on their sticks. The increased friction of roller hockey surfaces takes getting used to. You might find yourself skating past the puck if you try to keep it too close to your side.

As you perform the drills in this chapter, remember that these key points will greatly enhance your puck control skills, allowing you to enjoy success in your all-around game performance.

9 PUCK CONTROL WARM-UP

Purpose

To provide a warm-up that includes puck control skill development

Equipment

None

Time

4 to 6 minutes (about 60 to 90 seconds per quarter)

Procedure

1. Split rink evenly into four quarters.
2. Upon entering each zone, players perform predetermined tasks.
3. Players are in four groups that rotate to the next quarter at each whistle.

Key Points

- To save time, inform the players what activities they'll be doing *before* they go out for practice.
- Use visual or written task cards to reinforce activities in a specific location.

Drill Progression

- Add more activities per quarter while decreasing time allotted.

PUCK CONTROL WARM-UP 9

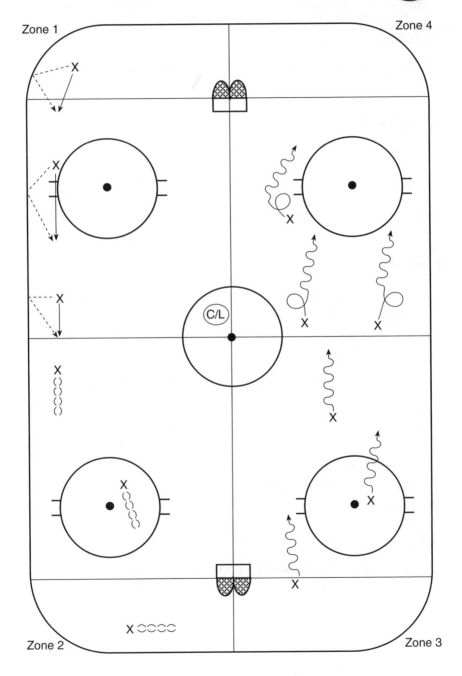

10 FACE THE FLAG

Purpose

To reinforce puck handling skills while skating either forward or backward

Equipment

None

Time

3 to 5 minutes, depending on skill level (four to six repetitions total)

Procedure

1. Always facing only one end of the rink, players skate around the five face-off circles.
2. Players pivot forward to backward and vice versa while controlling puck.
3. Players follow one another in a single line.

Key Points

- Players need enough room between them to recover in case of a mistake.
- If possible, demonstrate the route to help players visualize the activity.

Drill Progression

- Reduce time allowed to complete the activity.

FACE THE FLAG

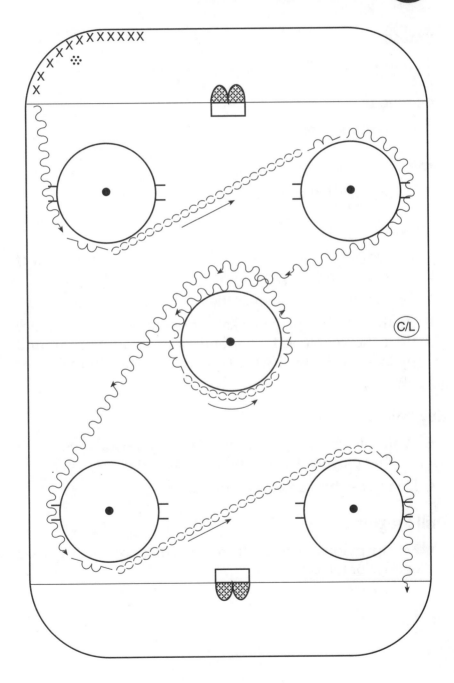

11 PYLON MADNESS

Purpose

To improve puck handling abilities while turning

Equipment

Pylons (and lots of them!)

Time

3 to 4 minutes (20 to 30 seconds each repetition)

Procedure

1. Players form two equal-sized groups, one at either end of the rink along the goal lines.
2. Distribute pylons all over the rink.
3. At the whistle, players skate forward, going no further than the center red line, and practice turning around pylons. At the next whistle, players return to their goal lines.

Key Points

- While players navigate the pylons, they must also be aware of other players. Heads and eyes should be up.
- Don't pass the center red line.

Drill Progression

- Set up pylons in a small, restricted space, such as one quarter of the rink.

PYLON MADNESS 11

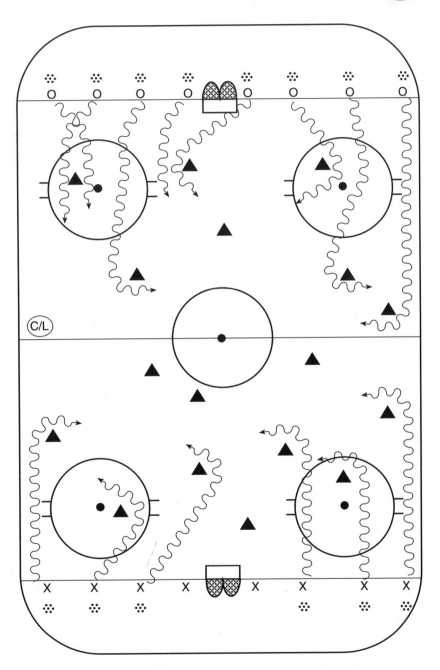

12 CIRCUIT

Purpose

To work on puck control and conditioning in a single activity

Equipment

A variety of apparatus, from pylons to sticks, skipping ropes to chairs

Time

2 minutes per station (1 minute per partner), with a 1-minute rest between partners

Procedure

1. Set up station areas on the rink surface based on group size.
2. Walk players through the stations, describing each activity, such as jumping rope while controlling a puck, stickhandling a puck through the legs of a chair, alternating between forward and backward skating around a face-off circle while controlling a puck, diving between the legs of a stationary partner while maintaining a puck on your stick, and so on.
3. A pair of players works at each station, beginning at the whistle.

Key Points

- Make activities as simple or complex as you wish.
- Include activities that help develop puck control.
- This is an exhausting drill, so players may need to rest.

Drill Progression

- Set up stations where three or four players participate.

CIRCUIT 12

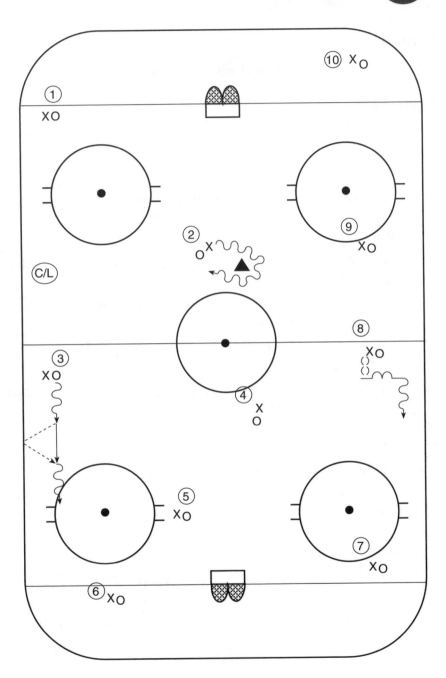

13 TURNCOAT

Purpose

To practice puck control skills under pressure

Equipment

None

Time

3 to 4 minutes (20 seconds per repetition)

Procedure

1. Using only half the playing surface, all players have a puck to control.
2. At the whistle, players attempt to knock the puck off of other players' sticks.
3. Each puck knocked off another player's stick earns one point.
4. You can assign players to teams, with total points counted and added for each squad.

Key Points

- Players are on their honor and keep their own score.
- Coach stays near center rink and supplies additional pucks to players if one goes over the center line.

Drill Progressions

- Have one group of puck handlers and one group of attackers with no pucks.
- Tighten the space parameters (e.g., reduce the rink by another half).

TURNCOAT 13

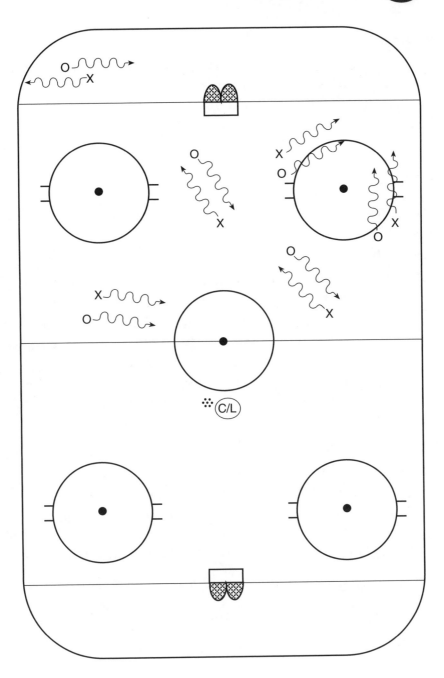

14 **THE RABBIT**

Purpose

To work on explosiveness in skating and puck control skills under game-like conditions

Equipment

None

Time

5 minutes

Procedure

1. Divide players into two equal groups in opposite corners of the rink.
2. At the whistle, the first player from each line skates as fast as he or she can to center, where the coach passes a puck.
3. Players compete for possession and finish with a shot on the net at the far end of the rink.

Key Points

- Players go only at the whistle.
- If a player loses the puck or is beaten to it, he or she must play defense, harassing the opponent.
- Once the drill is completed, players stay at the end of the rink where the shot was taken, and once all other players have gone, the drill starts from the opposite end.

Drill Progression

- Have players start from a variety of positions (knees, back, stomach).

THE RABBIT 14

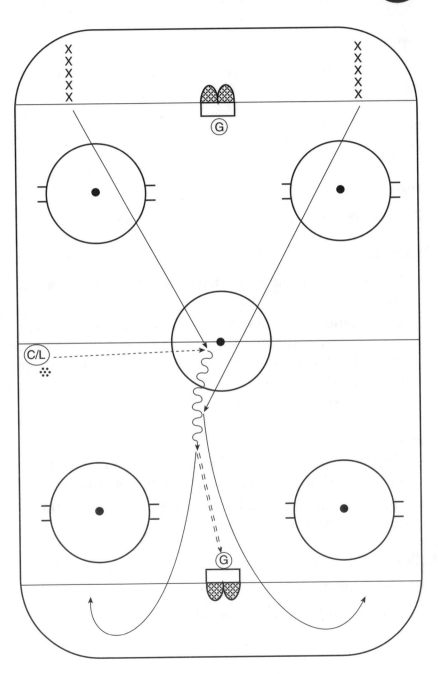

15 FACE THE MUSIC

Purpose

To practice puck control pressure drills in a noncontact situation

Equipment

None

Time

20 to 30 seconds per round (five rounds maximum)

Procedure

1. Players begin in pairs; the player with the puck uses a stick while the other cannot.
2. At the whistle, the player with possession tries to control the puck by putting it through the opponent's feet and around the body, while the defending player tries to steal the puck by using his or her skates.
3. At the next whistle, players switch roles.

Key Points

- Players must move around their opponent by using fakes, then immediately turn and face the opponent again.
- Limit players to a small area of the rink, forcing them to turn without much skating.

Drill Progressions

- Add limited contact to the drill.
- Allow both players to use sticks.

FACE THE MUSIC 15

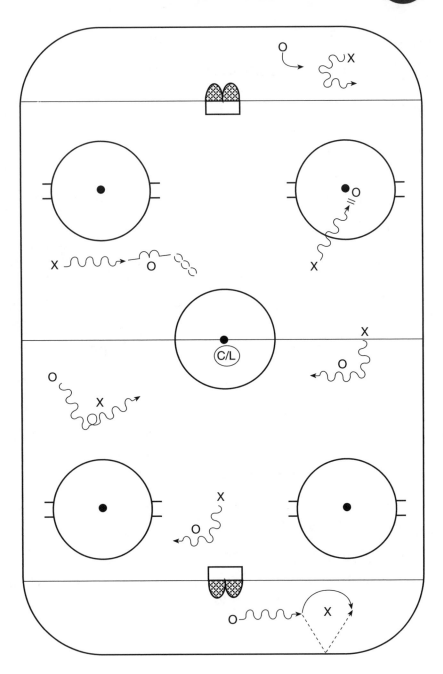

16 OFF THE HIP

Purpose

To practice using the body as a shield for puck protection

Equipment

None

Time

20 to 30 seconds per round (five rounds maximum)

Procedure

1. Players begin in pairs, one with a stick and puck, the other using only arms and hands.
2. Player with possession shields the opponent from the puck using his or her hips and trunk.
3. Players rotate their bodies to ward off opponents and maintain puck control.

Key Points

- Players stay in a small area of the rink so minimal skating is required.
- The player controlling the puck practices keeping arms extended.

Drill Progressions

- Have both players use sticks (as shown in photos).
- Form groups of three and force the player with the puck to rotate from one opponent to the other.

OFF THE HIP 16

17 PUCK CONTROL SHINNEY

Purpose

To develop puck control skills under pressure

Equipment

Pylons

Time

6 to 8 minutes (1 minute per round)

Procedure

1. Divide the rink into four quarters marked by pylons.
2. Each group of three or four players gets one puck.
3. Player with the puck controls it for as long as he or she can.
4. Players in all four quarters start at the whistle and stop on the next whistle (about 1 minute).
5. Players rest 45 seconds between each round.

Key Points

- Players maintain control of the puck by any legal means possible.
- Defensive players can only check with sticks—no body contact.
- Goalies should also participate to improve puck control skills.

Drill Progressions

- Allow minimum contact during the drill.
- Use two pucks at once.
- Reduce space.

PUCK CONTROL SHINNEY 17

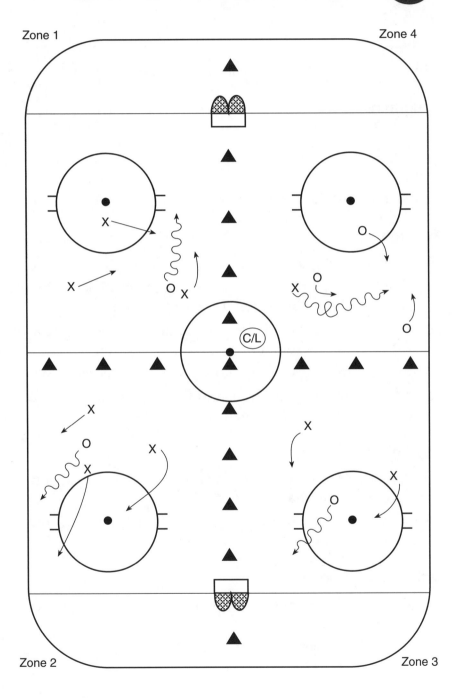

Zone 1

Zone 4

C/L

Zone 2

Zone 3

18 CORNER CRUNCH

Purpose

To practice puck control skills in a competitive situation

Equipment

None

Time

5 to 7 minutes (20 seconds per round)

Procedure

1. Coach begins drill by passing a puck into the corner.
2. The player who retrieves the puck attempts to maintain control and get to the net for a shot on goal.
3. Three defenders hold their zones and force the player with the puck to find openings.
4. Inactive players wait with the coach near center area.
5. At the whistle, play stops and the next group of players take their positions in the corner.

Key Points

- Player with the puck uses the boards, skates, or any other legal means to maintain control.
- Remind defensive players to try their hardest to make body contact with the puck carrier.

Drill Progressions

- To include passing in the drill, add another offensive player.
- Defensive players play without sticks.

CORNER CRUNCH 18

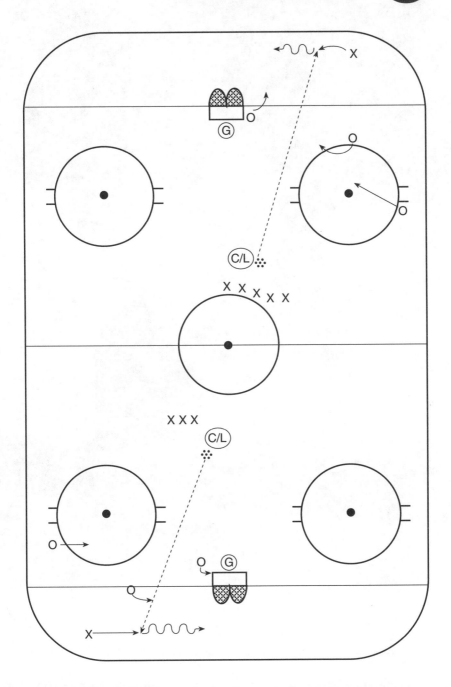

6

Passing
and Receiving

With no offside or icing calls in roller hockey rules, passing and receiving are central to successful strategies. Players who develop superior passing and receiving abilities will be at a great advantage over less skilled opponents who won't be able to capitalize on quick-break opportunities. Consider the following important points.

Passing

1. When passing, roller hockey players should learn to lead the receiver, meaning that passes should always be directed in front of the intended receiver. The exact location for the pass will depend on factors such as speed and distance from the target. Remember that the puck will begin to slow down on roller hockey surfaces over longer distances, so the target area needs to be moved somewhat further ahead in order to complete the pass.

2. Passes should not be sent behind the receiver—except in circumstances where the boards can be manipulated so that the puck bounces off the boards and continues toward the target. Normally it's best to pass ahead of the intended receiver so that the player can watch and be ready for any potential contact, incidental or otherwise. It is always easier to maintain momentum while skating forward as opposed to having to stop and/or turn to retrieve a puck passed behind you.

3. Players should avoid slapping at the puck when attempting to pass, as this can cause the puck to bounce excessively. A bouncing puck is difficult for the receiver to control and often causes a turnover. Quick, hard passes are the order of the day in roller hockey. Passes executed with a fluid motion are essential for proper passing on pavement.

Receiving

1. When receiving a pass, always present a target for the player passing the puck. Do this by keeping the blade of your stick flat on the playing surface and positioned where you want the puck delivered. Presenting a clear target helps the passer pass the puck in your direction and takes a lot of the guesswork out of the passing sequence. This simple technique will greatly increase your success in receiving a pass from teammates in any position on the playing surface.

2. Provide a "cushion" whenever receiving a pass to allow a small amount of recoil in the blade to help control the puck. If this technique is done properly, the stick will actually move slightly backward. When you keep the stick rigid and do not give with the wrists, you'll often see the puck bounce off the blade, making it very

difficult to keep possession. Learning how to accept a pass by using feel and soft hands takes a certain level of skill. By constantly practicing cushioning a pass, you'll soon see positive results in puck control and possession off a direct pass.

3. Learn to accept passes on both the forehand and backhand. Just as you need to execute skating skills going either forward or backward, you should also be able to receive a pass on either side of your stick blade. This will allow for increased control of the puck, especially off quick break opportunities, resulting in more scoring chances.

The passing and receiving drills found in this chapter represent a good cross section of activities, many of which may be attempted at either low or high tempo. Learning the proper mechanics first will ensure a smooth transition into higher levels of play. Practice these drills until both passing and receiving become automatic skills that can be easily executed.

19 PARTNER PASS

Purpose

To develop basic passing and receiving skills

Equipment

None

Time

3 to 4 minutes

Procedure

1. In pairs, players face each other and from a stationary position pass and receive the puck (forehand and backhand passes).
2. Players then skate across the width of the rink, the player with the puck skating forward and the partner backward, exchanging the puck as they go.
3. Players make a tight turn. As they come back in the other direction, the player who was skating forward now skates backward while the partner skates forward.

Key Points

- Players should spread out along the length of the rink to allow enough room for turning.
- Partners should be no more than 10 to 15 feet apart during this sequence.

Drill Progression

- Try one-time passing where the puck is not held but released immediately back to the partner.

PARTNER PASS 19

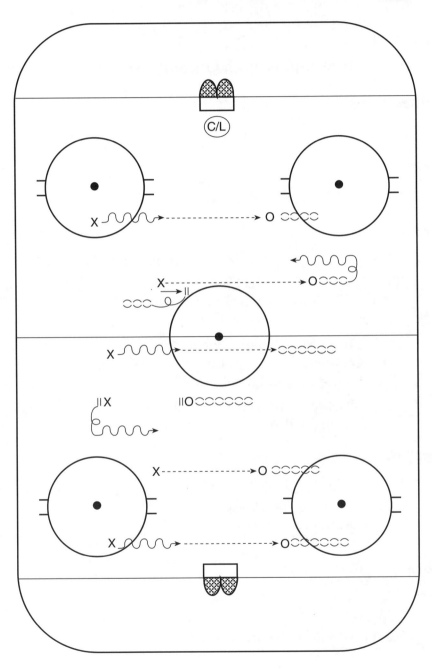

20 LINE PASS

Purpose

To practice passing the puck forward to a breaking teammate

Equipment

None

Time

5 to 7 minutes

Procedure

1. Players are in one of four lines at one end of the rink.
2. Player in Line 1 skates forward, receives a pass from Line 2, then continues forward to shoot on goal at the other end; player then stays at that end.
3. Player from Line 2 then receives a pass from Line 3, who in turn receives a pass from Line 4. The last pass is from Line 1 across the rink to Line 4.
4. Once all players are at the other end, the drill begins again in the opposite direction.

Key Points

- Roller hockey includes a lot of long, forward passing, which this drill simulates.
- Players must know which line will be passing to them.

Drill Progressions

- Add a pivot or turn at the beginning or middle of the sequence.
- Start out skating backward rather than forward.

LINE PASS 20

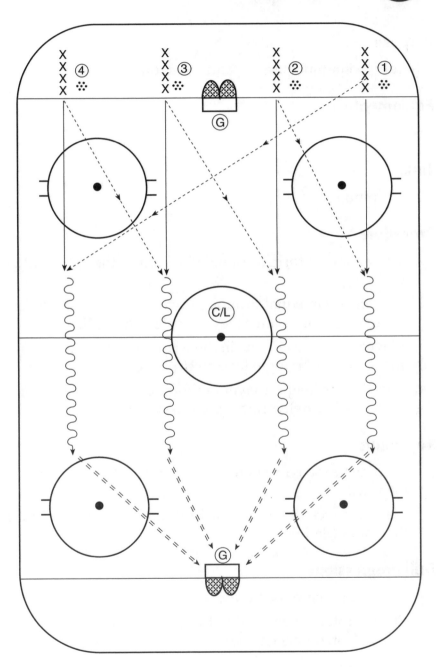

21 PASSING TRIANGLE

Purpose

To refine one-time passing and receiving

Equipment

None

Time

2 to 3 minutes

Procedure

1. Three players form a triangle in front of the net at either end.

2. Players are in equal groups in two corners, with players switching groups after they complete the drill.

3. Player passes to anyone in the triangle and skates around the top of the triangle for a return pass.

4. The three triangle players one-time pass among themselves before delivering a pass to skater.

Key Points

- All players focus on slightly tighter wrists to one-time pass the puck.

- Players concentrate on watching the puck onto and off their stick blade.

Drill Progressions

- Use one-touch passes only.

- Players rotate in and out of the triangle (i.e., shooter goes to one spot, others change).

PASSING TRIANGLE 21

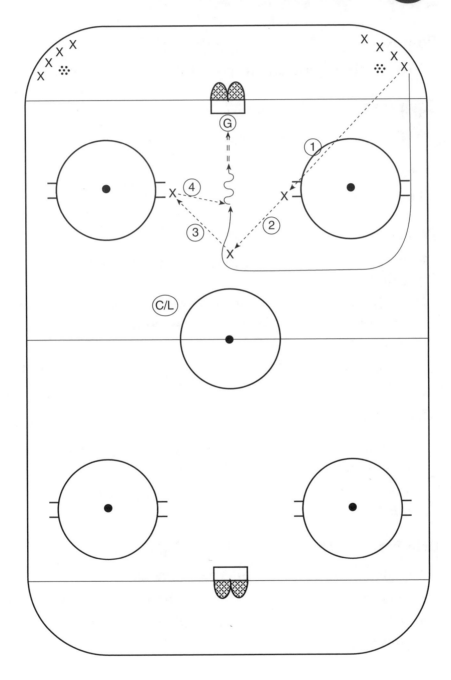

22 RUSSIAN WHEEL

Purpose

To develop passing and receiving skills at high speed

Equipment

None

Time

5 to 7 minutes

Procedure

1. Players begin in two even groups at opposite ends of the rink.
2. At the whistle, the first player from each line skates around the outer circle and receives a pass from the second player in the opposite group.
3. Player loops back to the end he or she came from and shoots on goal.

Key Points

- To make the drill continuous, the second player passing leaves immediately after the pass.
- Receiver should keep the stick down to provide a target for the passer.

Drill Progressions

- Split into four groups, alternating sides.
- Send two or three players rather than one.
- Add a defensive player who attempts to break up the attack.

RUSSIAN WHEEL 22

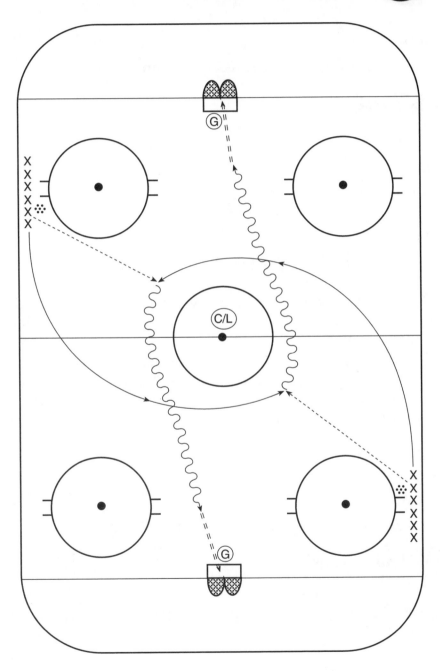

23 ONE-TOUCH SQUARE

Purpose

To practice long distance passing at high speed

Equipment

None

Time

4 to 5 minutes

Procedure

1. Divide players into four equal groups, one group in each corner of the rink.

2. At the whistle, two opposite lines begin (i.e., A and C), each skating to the red line with the puck and then passing to the next group.

3. After receiving a return pass, players circle the rink passing to and receiving the puck from each of the next two groups. Players finish the drill by shooting the puck at the net located at the end of the rink from which they began the drill.

Key Points

- Alternate sides with each whistle.
- Feet should keep moving throughout the drill.

Drill Progressions

- Try one-time passes to the next group.
- Begin next group while previous two players are still in motion.

ONE-TOUCH SQUARE 23

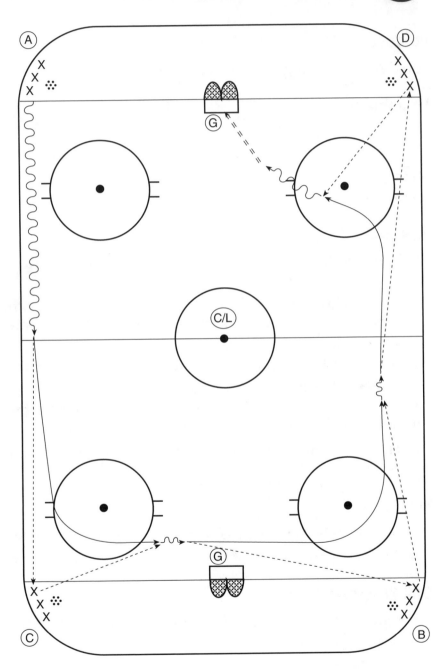

24 THREE-PASS KICKER

Purpose

To develop passing and receiving skills while on offense

Equipment

None

Time

4 to 5 minutes

Procedure

1. Split the team into two even groups, with each group assigned a player bench.
2. At the whistle, three players from each team come on the playing surface and pick up one puck from the center circle.
3. All three players from a team must touch the puck before a shot can be taken.
4. After a goal is scored the three players regroup at center rink, get a new puck, and go again.
5. The first team to have all three players score receives one point.

Key Points

- Require at least three passes before a goal can be scored.
- Keep a running count of the overall score for each team.

Drill Progressions

- Require all goals to be wrist shots one time, slap shots the next, and so on.
- Use one-time passes only.
- Add a defensive player from the other team.

THREE-PASS KICKER 24

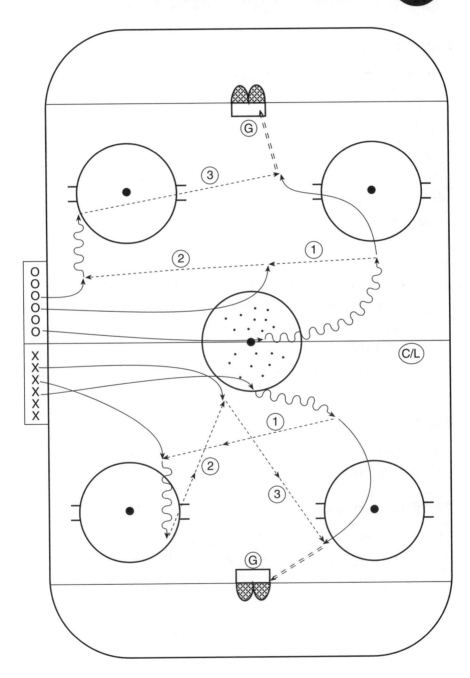

25 FOUR-ON-TWO FINISH

Purpose

To develop confidence in passing and receiving in an out-manned situation

Equipment

None

Time

5 to 7 minutes

Procedure

1. Forwards are in four lines at one end of the rink; defenders are at side boards near the middle of the rink.
2. Coach passes to first group of four players who attack against two defenders.
3. Play ends when a goal is scored or the goalie smothers the puck.

Key Point

- This drill should be done at game speed with an emphasis on quick puck movement.

Drill Progressions

- Add a late defensive forward to add pressure.
- Put a 10-second time limit on each attack.

FOUR-ON-TWO FINISH 25

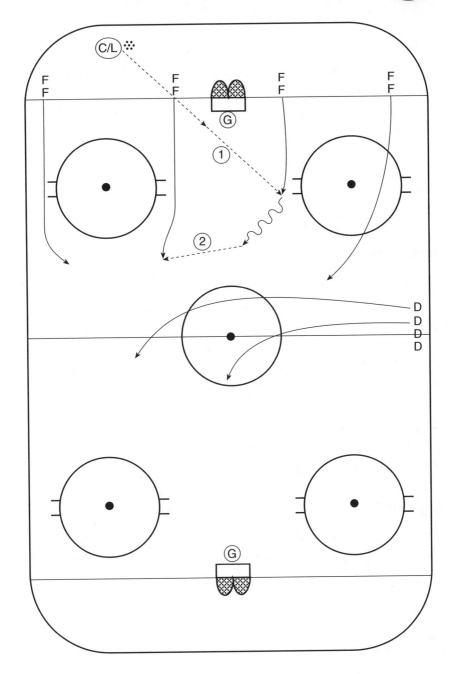

26 HOYER 2 BY 2

Purpose

To practice puck control at high speed while attacking the opposing team

Equipment

None

Time

3 to 4 minutes

Procedure

1. Groups of players position at each corner of the rink with pucks.
2. Play begins at the whistle at one end and a loop one-on-one is attempted (A).
3. On next whistle, a loop one-on-one starts at the other end, with the previous two players coming down the rink to make it a two-on-two (B).
4. Player on offense in the first part of the drill must be on defense in the second part.
5. Repeat pattern at the next whistle.

Key Points

- Perform this drill at high speed.
- Verbal communication is vital to help players identify their partner.

Drill Progression

- Do the drill three-on-three.

HOYER 2 BY 2 26

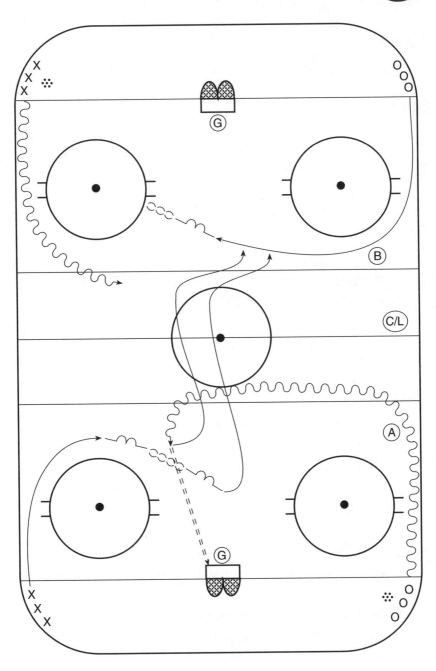

27 THREE-ON-THREE BATTLE

Purpose

To improve passing and receiving skills with resistance

Equipment

None

Time

5 to 6 minutes

Procedure

1. First three players in line go three-on-none, turn at other end, regroup, receive pass from coach, and come back toward the end where the drill started.

2. Second group of three players follow the first group to the red line, stop, and try to intercept any passes while skating backward.

Key Points

- Stress to the offensive players to make good passing decisions during execution.

- Defensive players try to block passing lanes and force bad passes.

- No contact is allowed.

Drill Progressions

- Add a puck to the initial rush so that shots are taken at both ends.

- Force second group of three (defensive players) to pick one player and lock, meaning that the defenders play a man-to-man defense which restricts opportunities for the attacking players.

THREE-ON-THREE BATTLE 27

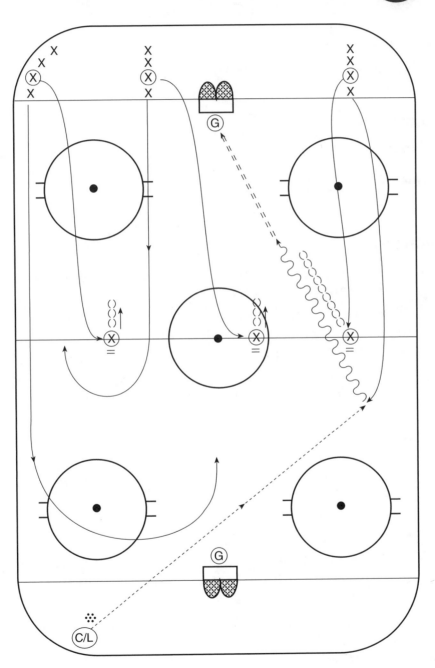

28 THREE-LINE RUSH

Purpose

To practice puck control at high speed under game-like conditions

Equipment

None

Time

40 to 60 seconds

Procedure

1. Defenders start on the players' bench; forwards are in one of three lines at either end of the rink.

2. The three lines on one end of the rink begin the drill by attacking three-on-none with no puck.

3. Players loop, receive a pass from Coach A, and one defender joins the drill from the bench creating a three-on-one the other way. Players take a shot on goal.

4. After the shot, Coach B passes another puck and two new defenders join the drill from the bench, creating a three-on-two situation.

5. Players conclude the drill with another shot on goal, completing the three-on-two attack.

Key Points

- After the line turns to finish with a three-on-two, the next line jumps in from the opposite end to begin the cycle again, going three-on-none, without a puck.
- Stress high speed.

Drill Progression

- Add backcheckers to the final two parts of the drill.

THREE-LINE RUSH 28

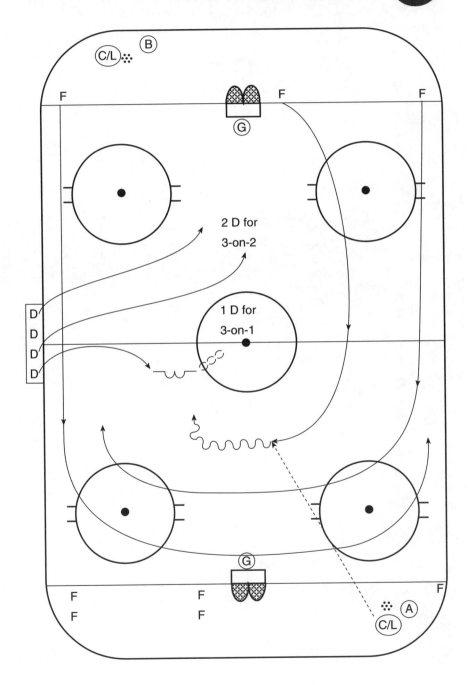

chapter

7

Shooting

Effective shooting in roller hockey is often affected by one key factor—a quick release. Here are some things to consider when working on a quick release:

1. A long wind-up or backswing is not advisable in roller hockey. As we discussed earlier, the puck will seem to "grab" roller hockey surfaces, which forces the puck carrier to set up and release the puck as quickly as possible. If enough forward speed has been generated, a player can actually skate past the puck if the release time is too long, resulting in no shot on goal and a possible turnover. Thus, quick release is a vital concern when players are in motion, and even more important when they are going at top speeds.

2. Players must commit to getting the puck on target as soon as possible, with "one-timing" off a pass an ideal strategy. One-timing refers to a player shooting the puck as it comes off a pass to the stick blade without delay—the puck is received and shot in one motion. This maneuver demands great concentration and a high skill level to execute properly. Like most other aspects of play, one-timing the puck requires hours of practice to achieve the intended results during the pressure of a game.

3. When in doubt in roller hockey, shoot the puck. Players at the professional level agree that given the opportunity to shoot or move in and fake out (deke) the goaltender during a scoring situation, it is usually best to shoot. And why not? Too much fancy stickhandling on roller surfaces almost inevitably leads to a turnover. Train yourself to get the shot on goal, then to follow that shot toward the net for a possible rebound. While the beautiful deke might work on occasion and put you on a highlight film, stress substance over style. The best advice for beginning roller hockey players is to work at improving your shooting through practice, and then to use this skill as an offensive weapon during game situations.

Roller hockey players use the same basic shots as in ice hockey, namely the wrist shot, the snap shot, the slap shot, and the backhand. Remember that developing proper mechanics is the most important key to effective shooting, and these techniques can be practiced almost as easily on the driveway as at the roller rink. What follows are some important basic mechanics that all players should understand and practice with each shot that they add to their shooting repertoire.

1. The puck should be located in the mid-blade area when shooting. This means that players should avoid having the puck either too far forward toward the toe of the blade or too far back toward the heel. By keeping the puck centered on the stick blade, greater accuracy is guaranteed.

2. Keep knees bent for maximum power and shift weight appropriately. Achieve greater speed in the shot by staying low and using your leg muscles to assist in shooting. Transfer body weight from the back to front leg when releasing any of the four shots.

3. For the hardest shot, load the cannon. The lower hand on the stick should slide down the shaft of the stick to generate more leverage and power in shooting. For left-side shooters, this would be the left hand; for right-side shooters, it will be their right hand. Try this at practice and you'll immediately notice a difference.

4. Follow through to the target. You'll often hear golfers complain that they didn't finish the shot by following through to the intended target. Hockey players often commit the same mistake. Focus on finishing your shot at the target—don't get "lazy arms" at the completion of the shot. Follow through high to put the puck in the "top shelf" of the net, or stay low to keep the puck in "the basement" or lower portions of the goal cage.

The following drills provide a variety of shooting challenges designed to improve release time and efficiency. Challenge players to continually improve the speed in which they execute these drills, and before long you'll have a team of shooting machines!

29 FULL RINK ROCKETS

Purpose

To develop long range shooting accuracy

Equipment

None

Time

3 to 4 minutes

Procedure

1. Four equal-sized groups begin in all four corners; pucks are in the center circle.

2. At the whistle, opposite corners go at the same time, skating to the opposite end and coming back to retrieve the puck in the middle.

3. Finish with a long shot on goal.

Key Points

- Keep feet moving at all times.
- Concentrate on getting the shot on target.

Drill Progressions

- Add a defensive player to follow the shooter.
- Shooters follow up for a rebound.

FULL RINK ROCKETS

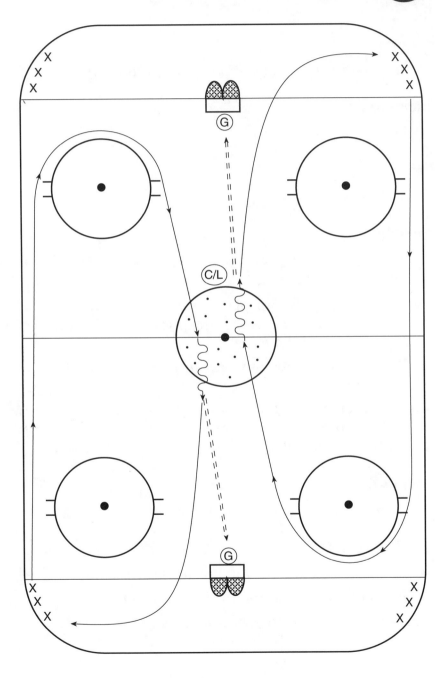

30 BOARD POPS

Purpose

To use boards in creating shooting opportunities

Equipment

Pylons

Time

4 to 5 minutes

Procedure

1. Two equal-sized groups line up on side boards facing the other side of the rink.
2. At the whistle, the first player in each line skates with puck toward a pylon and passes the puck off the boards while skating around the pylon.
3. Player retrieves puck and advances toward goal, finishing with shot.
4. The next player in line starts after the previous player has picked up his or her own board pass, thus making for continuous activity.

Key Point

- Players return to the line they started from.

Drill Progressions

- Have the second player in line feed pass.
- Start out skating backward and pivot at the pylon.
- Designate a variety of shots to try for each specific set.

BOARD POPS 30

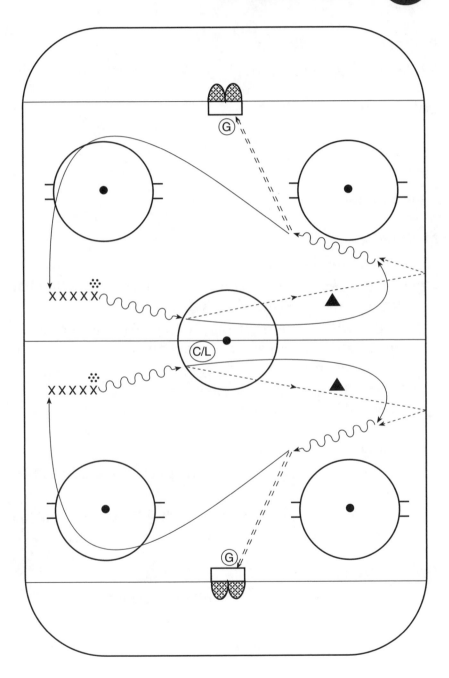

31 CIRCLE ATTACK

Purpose

To practice shooting through quick transition play

Equipment

None

Time

4 to 5 minutes

Procedure

1. Players start in the center circle.
2. Half the group skates in one direction while the other half skates in the opposite direction.
3. At the whistle the first player from each group skates quickly around the center circle and picks up a puck along the side boards.
4. A shot on target is released and the player follows for a second shot opportunity.

Key Points

- Keep feet moving and get to the puck as quickly as possible.
- This drill also provides goalies with shots from an outside angle, simulating game conditions.

Drill Progressions

- Players swing to puck from other direction.
- Add a defensive chaser for pressure.
- The player with the puck goes in for a deke.

CIRCLE ATTACK 31

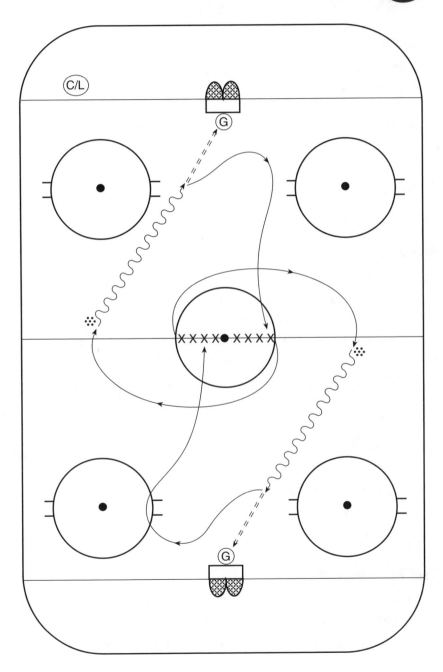

32 CENTER PIVOTS

Purpose

To maintain puck control off a pass and in situations that require a pivot

Equipment

' None

Time

2 to 3 minutes

Procedure

1. Divide players into four groups, one group each located along the boards between the center red line and face-off circle hash marks at either end.
2. Players skate out with stick blades on the playing surface; players from the other line pass to the sticks.
3. Players pivot and go, following the route shown.

Key Points

- Player receiving the pass has stick blade entirely on the playing surface.
- Turn 180 degrees during pivots.
- Pivot at bottom and top of end circle.
- Time the pass so that it will be received in the mid-rink area.

Drill Progressions

- Have players drop to their knees out of each pivot and get up as quickly as they can.
- At least once during the drill, use skates to control the puck.

CENTER PIVOTS 32

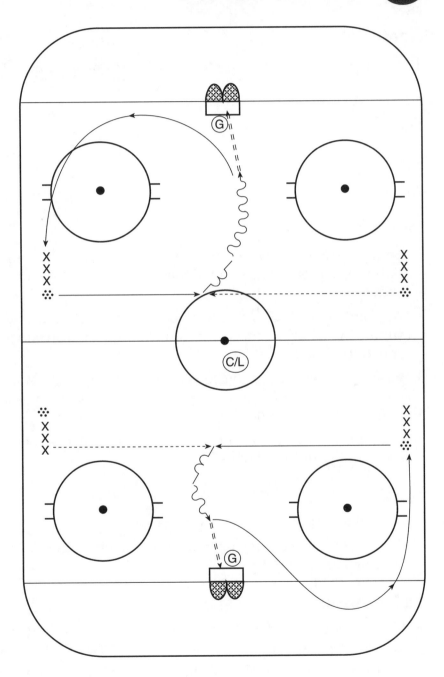

33 DENVER TIGHTS

Purpose

To practice shooting one-timers in a confined area

Equipment

None

Time

2 to 3 minutes

Procedure

1. Split players into four equal groups, one group each along the side boards near the top of the face-off circles at either end.

2. Appoint two players to act as passers at each end and situate them halfway between the net and boards on either side of their nets.

3. First player passes to player on goal line, skates toward net, receives a return pass, and shoots; player finishes by going to the back of the other line.

4. Next player comes from opposite group; players rotate accordingly until the whistle.

Key Points

- Keep the stick low and provide a target.
- Players try to release the shot immediately rather than holding and setting up.

Drill Progressions

- Players loop toward center and come down the middle for the return pass.
- Go from one side only, with the second group acting as rebounders, then switch lines.

DENVER TIGHTS 33

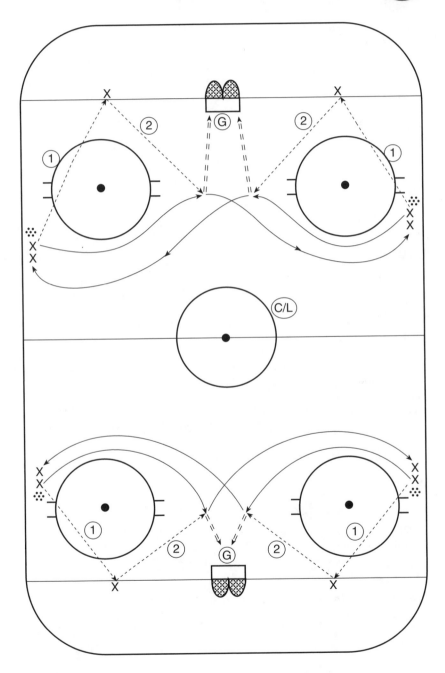

34 THREE SHOT DRILL

Purpose

To work on shooting from a variety of angles under time constrictions

Equipment

None

Time

3 to 4 minutes

Procedure

1. Split players into four equal groups, two at either end in the corners.
2. Player from one group starts with puck and loops into middle, firing a shot.
3. Player continues, pivoting backward, and receives a puck from the other group to shoot.
4. Player then makes another loop, pivots backward, and receives a third puck, this time from his own group, completing the drill.

Key Points

- Emphasize quick feet and quick release.
- Players concentrate on getting all three shots on target.

Drill Progressions

- Start backward and reverse the sequence.
- After the first shot, add a defensive player to shadow the shooter.

THREE SHOT DRILL 34

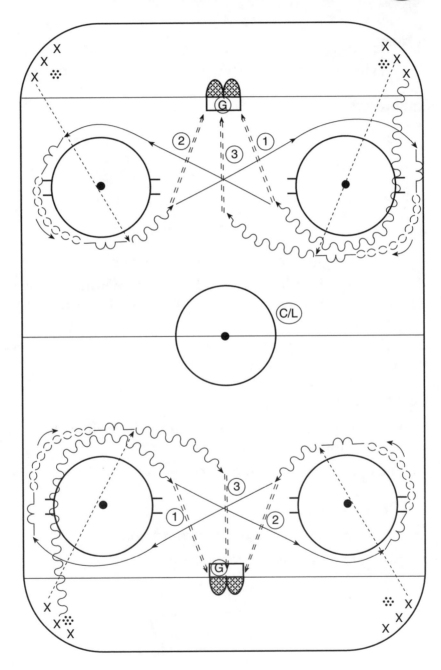

35 COACH'S CHOICE

Purpose

To practice following the shot for a second shot opportunity

Equipment

None

Time

4 to 5 minutes

Procedure

1. Players are in four even groups, one group in each corner.
2. At the whistle, players from opposite corners head toward the net and receive first puck from the opposite-corner group.
3. After shooting, player follows path to the net and receives second puck from coach in corner.

Key Points

- Work on getting the first shot on target early in order to position for second shot.
- Players attempt one-time shot for pass received from coach.

Drill Progressions

- Have two players go to net (two-on-none).
- Add late player as a defensive threat.

COACH'S CHOICE 35

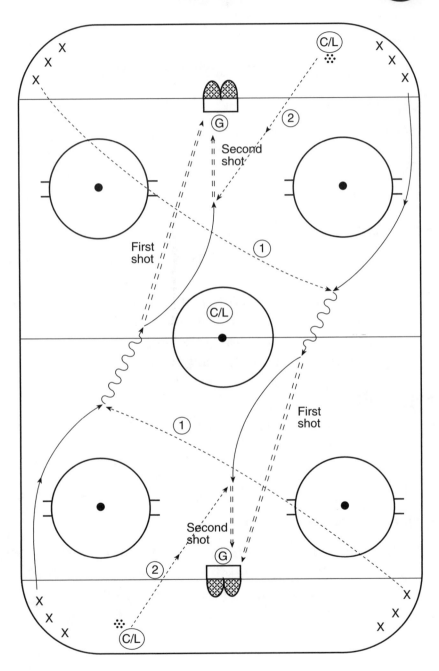

36 RED LINE DOWN

Purpose

To refine shooting technique while under pressure

Equipment

None

Time

2 to 3 minutes

Procedure

1. Two groups of players, each player paired with a partner, start at red line.
2. At the whistle, one player sprints with a puck to the net with his or her partner in pursuit.
3. Player shoots on goal and goes after the rebound, competing with the partner until the whistle is blown.

Key Points

- If the first shot is missed, the drill ends with a one-on-one in the corner.
- Give the player with the puck a two-step lead to start the drill.

Drill Progressions

- The defensive partner starts out facing the opposite direction of the puck carrier and must pivot before pursuing.
- Add a second offensive player for a two-on-one.
- Start from knees or stomach to work on foot speed.

RED LINE DOWN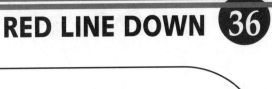

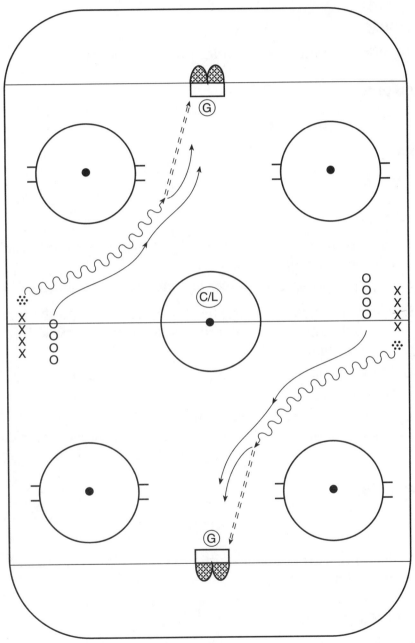

37 HITCH A RIDE

Purpose

To refine shooting skills under pressure and pursuit

Equipment

None

Time

5 to 6 minutes

Procedure

1. Players are in four equal-sized groups, one group in each corner with pucks.

2. Both ends, one side at a time, will start at the whistle.

3. The first player takes the puck around the top of the face-off circle and shoots, continues skating, and picks up a second puck.

4. The next player in line pursues and harasses player all the way to the net.

5. Puck carrier must avoid pursuing player and other two players from opposite end who enter the center circle at the same time.

Key Points

- If the defensive player steals the puck, he or she becomes the shooter.

- Players control the puck while keeping their heads up and eyes on their opponents.

Drill Progression

- Add another player to make the drill a two-on-one situation for the second shot.

HITCH A RIDE 37

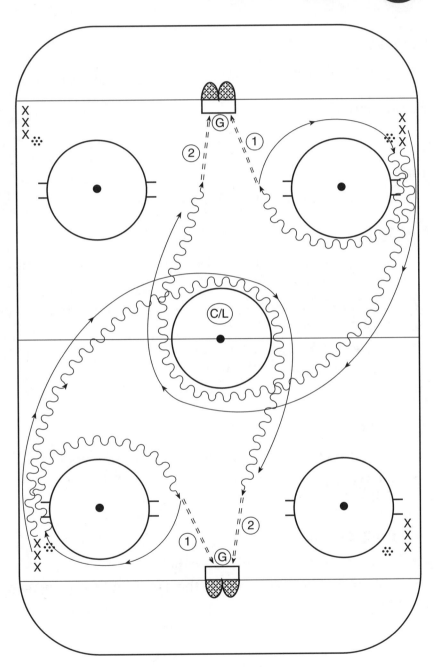

38 BULLDOG

Purpose

To practice shot release under extreme pressure

Equipment

None

Time

5 to 6 minutes (20 to 30 seconds per round)

Procedure

1. One player stands facing the goal with multiple pucks around the net.
2. At the whistle, three defensive players attempt to prevent the shooter from scoring.
3. Shooter must keep in motion and try to shoot as many pucks as possible while being defended.
4. Play continues at both ends until the whistle blows.

Key Points

- Shooter focuses on quick release and quick feet.
- Defensive players do their best to restrict shooting opportunities.

Drill Progressions

- Remove sticks from defensive players.
- Add a support player behind the net who passes pucks for shooter.

BULLDOG 38

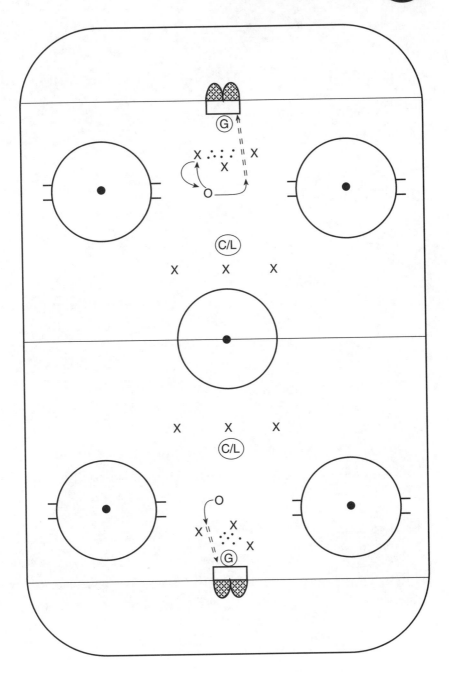

chapter

8

Goaltending

Of all the positions available in the world of sports, few compare with being a goaltender. Whether the sport is water polo, roller hockey, or soccer, goaltending is a technique position requiring years of practice to master. Specific to roller hockey, a goalie faces unique peculiarities that must be appreciated for the position to be perfected.

1. To effectively handle duties "between the pipes," goaltenders must be aware of some basics common to the position. One of the most important involves goaltender responsibilities during an opponent's attack. Most teams play some form of defensive system where the goalie's primary duty is to stop any first shot opportunities. This means that the goalie must always be set and square to the

shooter, focusing primarily on stopping the puck carrier. Teammates should then position to clear any potential second strike chances. If a goalie can't save a high percentage of first shot opportunities, the chances for a team victory are greatly reduced.

2. Goaltenders most constantly work to improve in controlling rebound opportunities, a technique that takes much time and practice to perfect. Most quality goaltenders develop sound catching and blocking techniques through the course of their maturation at the position, which allows them to reduce the number of second or third shot chances arising from rebounds. If a goaltender hopes to move into the elite levels of play, this skill must be refined.

3. When moving quickly from one side of the goal to the other, roller goalies fight the friction between the side of their skate wheels and the playing surface. Thus, they must pay special attention to the position of their lead foot when attempting to move across the goal crease. Otherwise, the goalie's skate will catch on the playing surface and he or she will end up in a heap!

4. Goaltenders in ice hockey are constantly told to challenge the shooter by using a technique called telescoping. In telescoping, the goalie comes out of the net to cut down the shooting angle for the attacking player. The problem for roller goalies is that once they come out, friction makes it very difficult for them to recover back into the net. Again, the skate wheels and playing surface are not as friction-free as skates on ice, and roller goalies must always remember this simple fact.

5. In roller hockey, transition is a vital component of play, and goaltenders must be able to contribute to this facet of the game. They should constantly work at their puck-handling skills, especially passing both short and long distances. A goaltender who can contribute these kinds of skills to a team can be a great advantage, and any player who occupies this position should be included in practice drills that improve overall puck control skills.

6. One of the qualities associated with successful goalies is their leadership under pressure. Goalies should work during practice to develop this quality by constantly communicating with their teammates, who usually can't see as much of the playing surface. Often a goaltender can act as a quarterback while teammates are in their defensive zone by helping to identify where an attack is coming from,

as well as positioning players for proper defensive coverage or break-out sequences.

The drills and activities included here will test all goaltenders, regardless of their skill level. Whether you're practicing foot speed, working on handling the puck with efficiency, or developing up-and-down technique, these drills will ensure that roller goalies are included in practice drilling and pushed to improve.

39 HORSESHOE

Purpose

To give goalies various shots to defend from multiple angles

Equipment

None

Time

2 to 4 minutes (5 to 6 rounds of shots)

Procedure

1. Players assemble with pucks in a U-formation around the goalie.
2. First player shoots, second player comes in and dekes, next player shoots, and so on.

Key Points

- Make sure that the next shooter ready to fire doesn't begin until the goalie is set.
- The U-shaped line of players can start far out and move gradually closer to the goalie with each succeeding round.

Drill Progression

- Start from the left side, then have the second shot (or deke) come from the right, forcing the goalie to move across the goal mouth.

HORSESHOE 39

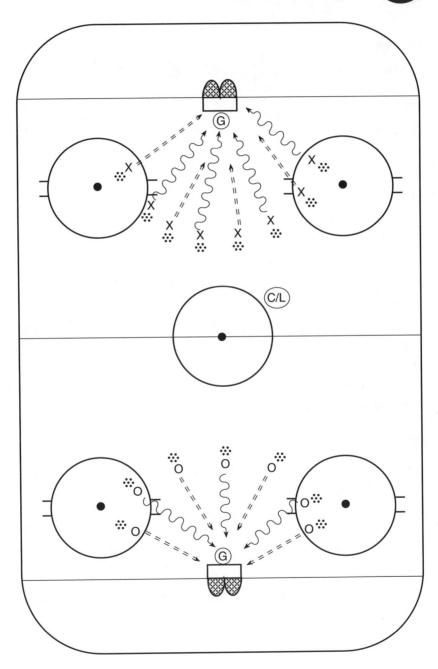

133

40 RAPID FIRE

Purpose

To allow goalies to see multiple shots from the same angle as a means of warming up and positioning

Equipment

None

Time

2 to 3 minutes

Procedure

1. Players are in two equal groups in opposite corners of the rink.

2. At the whistle, players skate toward the far end and shoot in rapid succession on the goalie from roughly the same spot.

3. Players finish by going to the corner where they wait to reload.

Key Points

- Goalies feel the puck on the pad/gloves, which prepares them for practice.

- Goalies can adjust angles.

Drill Progression

- Position goalie at different depths relative to shooters, sometimes deep in the crease, other times telescoping out further.

RAPID FIRE 40

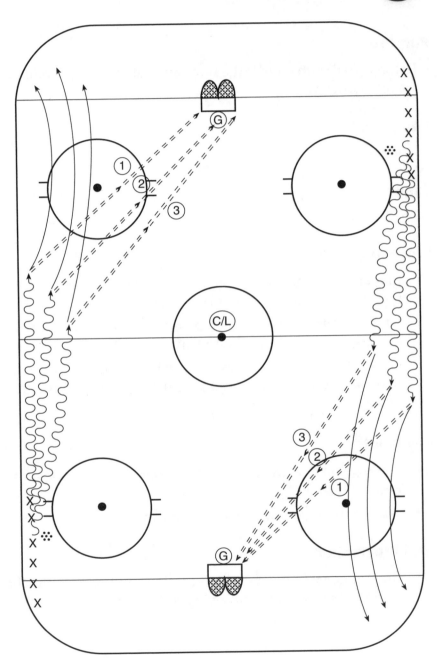

135

41 GET THE HANDLE

Purpose

To force goalies to handle the puck and set up behind their net for breakout

Equipment

None

Time

4 to 5 minutes

Procedure

1. Players locate in two groups near the center red line with half of each group facing opposite ends.
2. At the whistle, one player passes the puck around the boards, forcing the goalie to leave the net to stop it.
3. Opposite player retrieves the puck and starts a two-on-none rush with the original passer in the other direction.
4. The same sequence occurs at opposite end of the rink.

Key Points

- Goalies first stop the puck and then set it in a good position for easy retrieval.
- Goalies then face two-on-none coming from other end.

Drill Progression

- The winger dumps the puck directly on the net and the goalie passes to a breaking player.

GET THE HANDLE 41

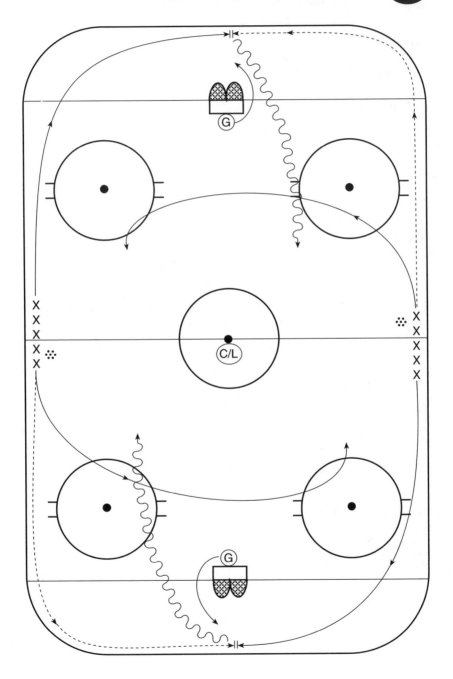

42 GOALIE WIDE RUN

Purpose

To practice passing the puck for distance around the boards

Equipment

None

Time

2 to 3 minutes

Procedure

1. Players stand along both side boards in two equal groups; coaches have the pucks in the center circle.
2. At the whistle, the coach directs pucks into either end; goalies first control the puck, then release it to a waiting player along the boards.
3. Drill finishes with a full rink one-on-zero.

Key Points

- Transition is a key part of roller hockey—goalies must be able to control and move the puck up quickly.
- When on the backhand, goalies can go short or long side.

Drill Progression

- Add an attacking player to force the goalie to move the puck quickly.

GOALIE WIDE RUN

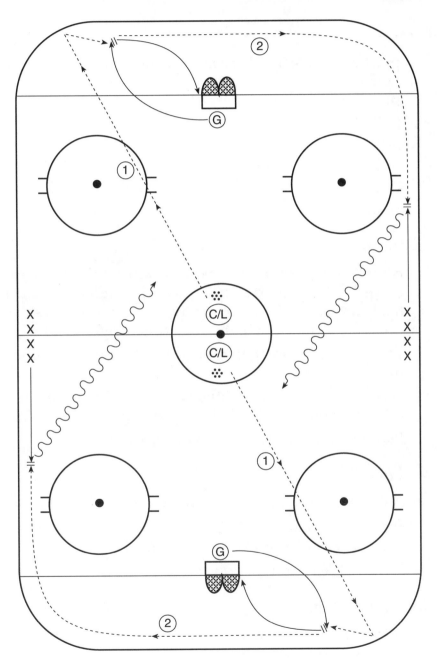

43 KILLER'S BUMP

Purpose

To practice puck control for goalies and team transition to offense

Equipment

None

Time

3 to 4 minutes

Procedure

1. Alternate the end of the rink from which the drill starts. Players will exit the bench in groups of three and re-enter the bench area after finishing the drill. This ensures that everyone is involved in the activity equally.
2. Three players jump from the bench as the puck is directed by coach on net.
3. Goalie controls puck and then passes to designated area near the center red line where a forward is positioned.
4. Play a three-on-none to finish the drill.

Key Points

- Player taking the pass near the center red line stays in motion.
- The next group receives the pass from the other goalie.
- Try to move the puck as quickly as possible.

Drill Progressions

- Add two or three defenders as backcheckers once the puck passes the red line.
- Go two full units (four-on-four).

KILLER'S BUMP 43

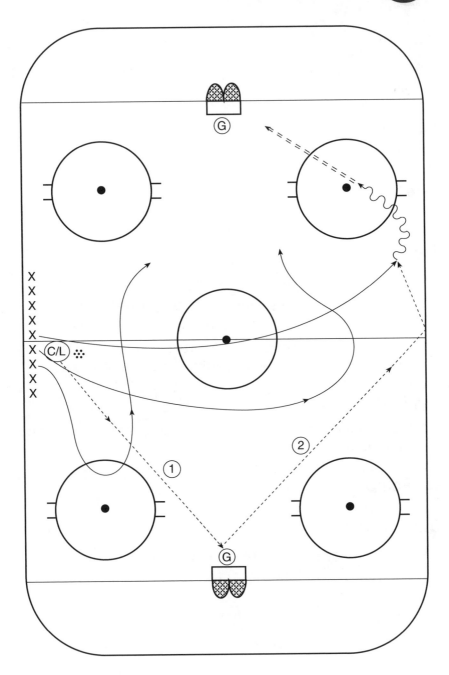

44 TIP TIME

Purpose

To provide goalies with practice in passing the puck on breakouts and learning to control tip shots

Equipment

None

Time

5 to 6 minutes

Procedure

1. Players are in equal-sized groups in all four corners.
2. At the whistle, the goalie at either end goes to the back of the net, retrieves the puck, and passes to a player.
3. The goalie must then quickly return to the net to face a long shot/pass and tip from the other side of the cage.

Key Points

- Goalies focus first on handling the puck before attempting to re-enter the net.
- Any tips or deflections should be stopped and then covered to prevent further scoring chances.

Drill Progression

- A stationary player takes an extra shot in the neutral zone area for a second tip.

TIP TIME 44

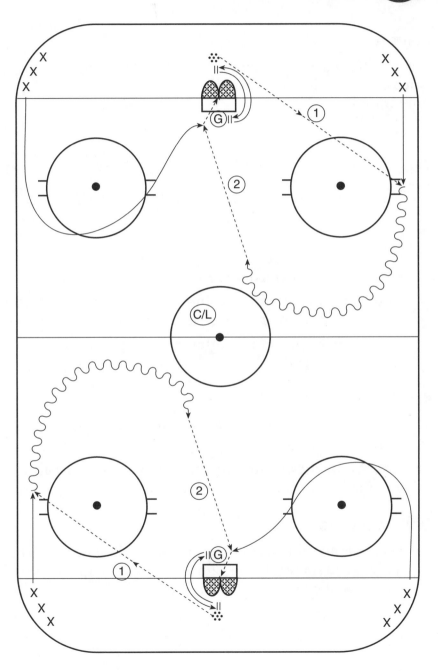

45 SCREEN DOOR

Purpose

To practice fighting through screen shots to make a save

Equipment

None

Time

2 to 3 minutes

Procedure

1. Three players line up to block the goalie's vision on a shot that will come from out high.

2. The player in the corner (both ends) makes a turn with the puck near the center red line and shoots a low shot on net.

3. As the puck gets through, the screening players turn and move in for rebounds.

Key Points

- Goalies move up and down or laterally to position and then see the puck.

- Goalies attempt to stop initial shot and not give any rebounds.

Drill Progression

- Have another puck come from a passer behind the net to the original shooter in the high slot area, setting up a second screen by the three players in front.

SCREEN DOOR 45

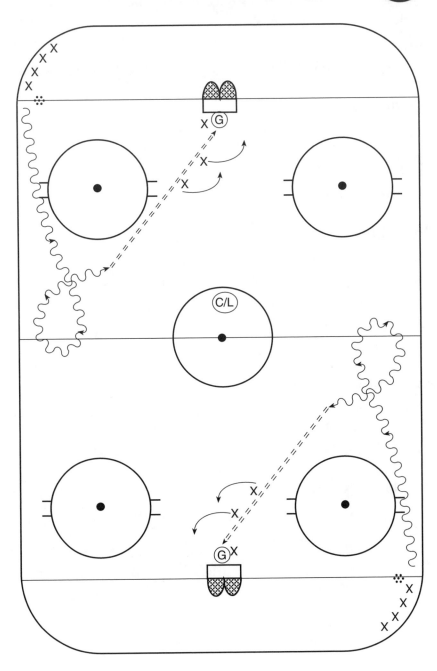

46 THREE SHOT FEVER

Purpose

To practice moving side to side within the goal crease area

Equipment

None

Time

5 to 7 minutes

Procedure

1. Players form three lines at each end of the rink.
2. At the whistle, the middle line shoots, followed by the second line, and finally the third line.
3. Goalies make each save and then quickly get across the crease to prevent any goals from subsequent shooters.

Key Points

- Goalies practice pushing off their feet to cover the second and third shots.
- Double-pad stack saves should be tried on the third shot.

Drill Progression

- Having a rebounder on either side of the net forces goalies into second-shot saves.

THREE SHOT FEVER

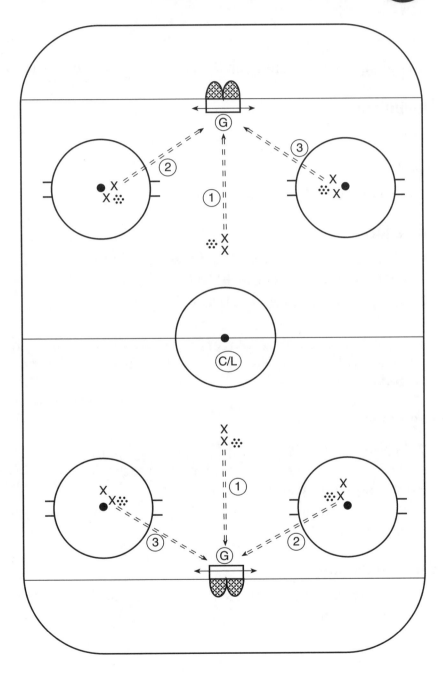

47 CENTER SCRAMBLE

Purpose

To train goalies in picking up the puck behind or beside them

Equipment

None

Time

7 to 10 minutes (30 seconds per shift)

Procedure

1. Players form two equal-sized teams and line up near the center of the rink, about 40 feet apart.
2. Place two nets back to back with a 10-foot gap between them.
3. Each team sends three players at the whistle for a three-on-three drill, with goalies forced to check behind for players and puck location.

Key Points

- Coach replaces stray pucks.
- At the whistle, three new players from each team enter play (should be continuous play).
- Players waiting to get in can help their team as outside passers.

Drill Progression

- Have goalies change nets with every whistle, forcing them to work on quickness.

CENTER SCRAMBLE

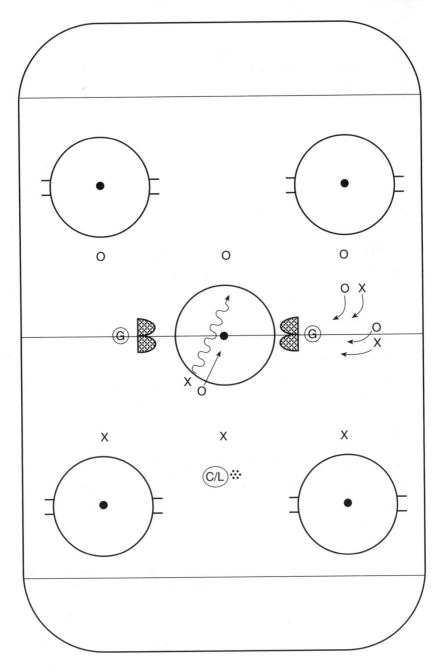

48 ANGLE SHOWDOWN

Purpose

To prepare goalies for one-on-one confrontations with attacking players

Equipment

None

Time

7 to 10 minutes

Procedure

1. Players form two groups on either side board near the center red line.
2. At the whistle, one player from each line skates to the center circle, retrieves a puck, skates in on the goalie, and tries to score.
3. At the next whistle, two more players go but cannot attack from the same angle as the previous shooter.

Key Points

- Goalies work at stopping players from a variety of angles.
- Goalies learn to first read the attack angle, then set for position.

Drill Progression

- Position a rebounder off to the side of the net who will pounce on any second shot chances.

ANGLE SHOWDOWN

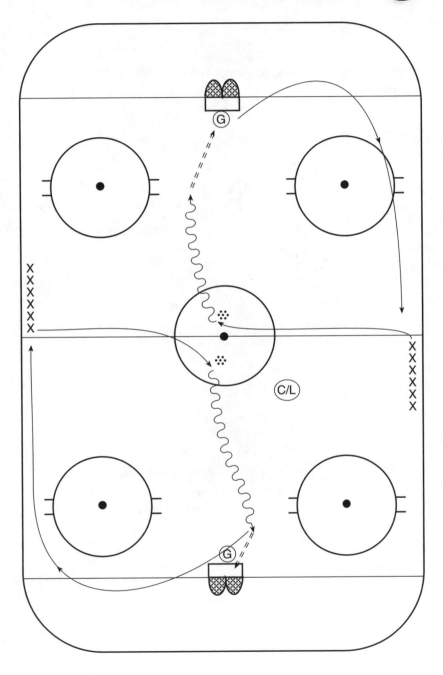

9

Offensive Team Strategies

Up to now, we have focused on individual skills that roller hockey players must master to play the game well. The ensuing chapters will focus on team-related concepts and principles of play that guide successful roller hockey programs. Included are sections that examine offensive tactics, transition play, and defensive strategies. While some of the information might be advanced for players and teams just starting out in the game, the basic ideas are useful in virtually any roller hockey scenario. In chapters 9 through 11 you will find drilling patterns that reinforce the main themes found in roller hockey team strategies.

This chapter highlights offensive concepts guided by the three central principles that follow:

- **Principle #1: Move the puck forward quickly!** The best defense is a good offense, so work at moving the puck to the offensive zone as quickly as possible, either by skating or passing.

- **Principle #2: Be proactive.** Don't just read and react to game situations. Learn to anticipate and move accordingly.

- **Principle #3: Use width and depth.** Incorporate these at the center of your offensive tactics and practice.

Roller hockey presents many options for playing styles and tactics when on the attack. The four-on-four format of this game makes for a wide-open and exciting activity with many opportunities to go on the offensive and score goals. First, let's examine the three key principles of offensive play just listed; then we'll diagram some practice activities that reinforce these concepts.

Principle #1: Move the Puck Forward Quickly!

Roller hockey is a skill game, and offense is a key component of the skills required to play at a high level. Included in this section are various concepts illustrated through drilling patterns designed to reinforce sound offensive play. Several key components are essential to reinforcing this first principle of roller hockey strategy, and they are demonstrated through this principle's accompanying drills. Note that many players accustomed to ice hockey rules and etiquette will instinctively hold back near an imaginary offensive blue line in case of an offsides call. But roller hockey has no offsides or icing calls. Since they cannot go offside, players must train themselves to forget where the different lines are located and concentrate on accelerating into the offensive zone, rather than slowing down.

Principle #2: Be Proactive

The game of roller hockey is structured so that gaps and lanes of space are open for players who can quickly analyze situations. By being proactive and initiating the attack, players and teams are much more likely to succeed on the offensive side. Things happen quickly in this game—players need to be drilled so they recognize offensive chances and capitalize on them.

Principle #3: Use Width and Depth

In many sports you hear coaches telling athletes to use more of the court, field, or rink when attacking an opponent. By spreading out your offensive players, you force defenders to spread out as well, which allows openings for skilled players to exploit. Avoid having multiple players working in a relatively small space, as this is too easy to defend. Instead, drill players to use the entire playing surface to create offensive opportunities.

The drills that follow focus on offensive tactics and reinforce the three basic principles just discussed. As players and teams become more advanced in their skills and strategy, you can design and use variations of these drills to match changing skill levels.

49 ONE-ON-ONE FULL RINK

Strategy

During one-on-one play try to use either outside-in or inside-out moves depending on whether the attacker or defender has the advantage. Attacking players who have a step on the defender should stay wide (outside) and use speed to beat the defender before cutting into the middle of the rink toward the net. Conversely, when the defensive player has shut down the outside option, offensive players might be more effective by faking the outside move and following it with a cut-back move to the inside position. Both moves should be practiced and mastered, eventually at high speed.

Procedure

1. Forwards form two groups at either end of the rink; defensive players form two groups at either side of the red line.

2. On the whistle, one forward from each group takes a puck from behind the net and attacks a defender one-on-one, seeking to gain an advantage either inside or outside during the rush.

3. Once the offensive rush is completed, players switch groups—attacking players become defenders while defenders go on the attack.

Key Points

- Attacking players keep their feet moving to generate speed at point of attack.

- Forwards practice shoulder, head, and stick fakes.

- Forwards learn to tell when they have an advantage over the defender and how to take advantage.

- To simulate game conditions, players should attempt to both attack and defend.

ONE-ON-ONE FULL RINK 49

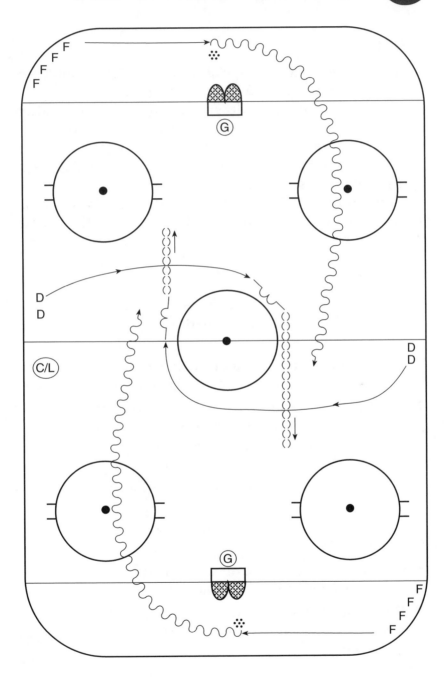

50 TWO-ON-ONE ATTACK

Strategy

When playing a two-on-one, attacking players should consider two main offensive options. In one option, the player without the puck slows down and joins the attack after a slight delay, allowing the puck carrier to choose to shoot on net or drop the puck back to the late attacker. The second option is to send the player without the puck hard to the net and simultaneously allow the puck carrier to cut across the playing surface, using the partner without the puck as a screen for shooting. In either option, communication is essential for proper execution.

Procedure

1. Forwards form four groups near the face-off circles at either end; defenders are equally divided on either side of the center red line.

2. When the coach directs a puck on net, the goalie passes to one of two forwards who have looped into the zone.

3. After a defender jumps into play, forwards proceed on a two-on-one. When finished, forwards join one of the two groups of forwards at the same end.

4. After the attack has been completed, the next pair of forwards skate from the other end of the rink, and the drill begins again.

Key Points

- Forward with the puck decides whether to attack the net and shoot or pass to teammate.

- The player without the puck decides whether to go hard toward the net or slow down and release to the middle area of the rink.

- Both forwards finish at the net for any rebounds.

TWO-ON-ONE ATTACK

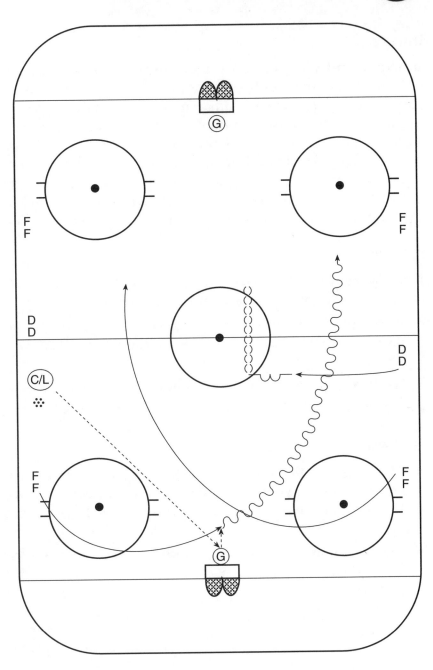

51 OPTION THREE-ON-TWO

Strategy

In a three-on-two situation the attacking players have several options. Many coaches treat this offensive opportunity as an expanded two-on-one, making it a progression during practice drills. As in the two-on-one, the puck carrier always has the first option to shoot. With the extra attacker, however, the puck carrier gains an additional option. He or she can shoot, pass to a teammate driving through the middle toward the net, or pass to the third linemate, who can either skate hard to the far post of the net or drop into the middle as a late trailer.

Procedure

1. Forwards form three groups at one end of the rink; defenders split into two groups near the red center line.

2. After the coach directs the puck on the net, the goalie passes to one of three forwards, initiating the three-on-two.

3. As the forwards leave, two defenders jump in to play.

4. When finished, players join their original groups.

Key Points

- Forwards practice variations of the breakout, sometimes coming out relatively close together, other times stretching the defenders by sending one or more players deep into the attacking zone.

- Forwards maintain possession until a good scoring chance is available.

OPTION THREE-ON-TWO

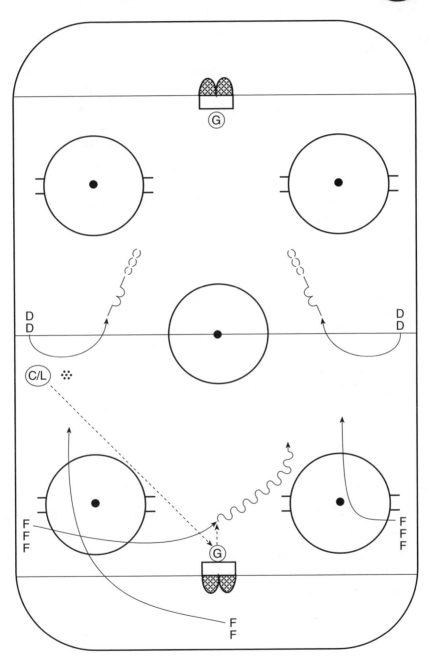

52 CYCLING

Strategy

Practicing cycling of the puck in the offensive zone forces players to become more proactive in getting to specific areas of the playing surface more quickly. Using two or three players, the offensive team can be drilled at using the boards to back pass the puck to a teammate, followed by all players without the puck skating in a counterclockwise fashion. The purpose for this rotation is to shake off a defender and create an open area of playing surface that players can exploit for prime scoring chances.

Procedure

1. Players are divided into 2 equal groups, one at either end of the rink, forwards and defenders together.
2. Coach will put a puck into the corner with three players attempting to cycle against one defender.
3. Once an attacking player has a prime scoring chance a shot is taken, rebounds are played for secondary scoring opportunities.
4. Continue cycling drill in either corner until coach blows the whistle to finish the drill.

Key Points

- The attacking players must be proactive and get into position before a cycled pass is made.
- Players must show patience and not shoot from poor scoring angles, as cycling is designed to control the play and generate grade A chances.
- Players should be attackers once, then play the defending role as well.

CYCLING 52

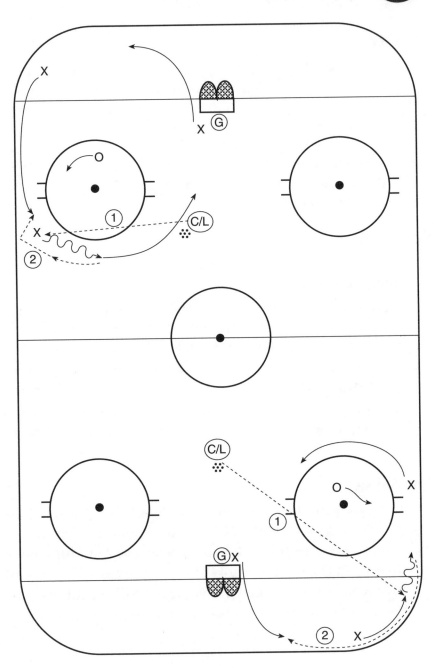

53 BACK DOOR FEED

Strategy

Once a player has released the puck to a teammate, he or she attempts to position near the net where a scoring chance is likely if the puck is returned. By passing off and moving behind the net, offensive players can sometimes "get lost"— that is, defenders lose track of where they are. Players can then position themselves off to the side of the net to wait for a pass that results in a grade A scoring chance. This drill is a natural progression from the cycling drill just described (#52).

Procedure

1. Divide the team into two equal-sized groups, one at either end of the rink.

2. Give one of three attacking players a puck; this player moves the puck along the boards to a teammate before moving into the high slot area, looking for a return pass.

3. The attacker positioned behind the net releases the puck (cycles) and moves to the side of the net opposite the puck.

4. The player with the puck can pass high to the slot area or go backdoor to the teammate positioned at the side of the net.

Key Points

- If possible, the backdoor player delays behind the net long enough to be forgotten or lost by the defending team. He or she then moves off to the goalie's side to wait for a cross pass or plays any rebound from a slot shot.

- If play fails, the attacking players can work an automatic to the back of the net.

BACK DOOR FEED 53

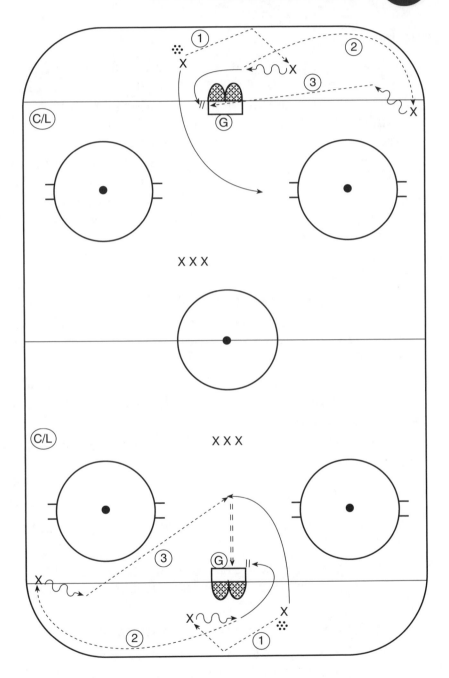

54 WIDE RIM TIP

Strategy

Sometimes a player cannot make a pass directly on to a teammate's stick. In the following drill, the puck carrier is receiving considerable defensive pressure and attempts a wide rim pass to a teammate on the other side of the rink. This is done by passing the puck along the boards and letting it follow the contour of the rink, arriving on the stick of an awaiting teammate. The passer then heads to the net for a possible tip in. Once the wide rim pass has been made, the players without the puck move into scoring positions for a pass, tip in, or rebound.

Procedure

1. Players form two equal groups at either end of the rink.
2. A coach initiates the play by directing a puck into the corner. The closest attacker retrieves the puck while under pressure from a defensive player.
3. The puck carrier fires a hard pass around the outside boards to a teammate inside the center red line, then skates to the side of the net.
4. A shot is directed toward the net, with the original passer attempting a tip in.

Key Points

- The original wide rim pass must be firm to make it all the way around.
- After the initial pass, the passer moves quickly to the side of the net for an expected shot or pass from the player with puck possession.
- Other players keep sticks low to the surface and move into position to capitalize on any rebound opportunities.
- Player shooting the puck takes something off the shot—it is really a hard pass, not an attempt to score.

WIDE RIM TIP 54

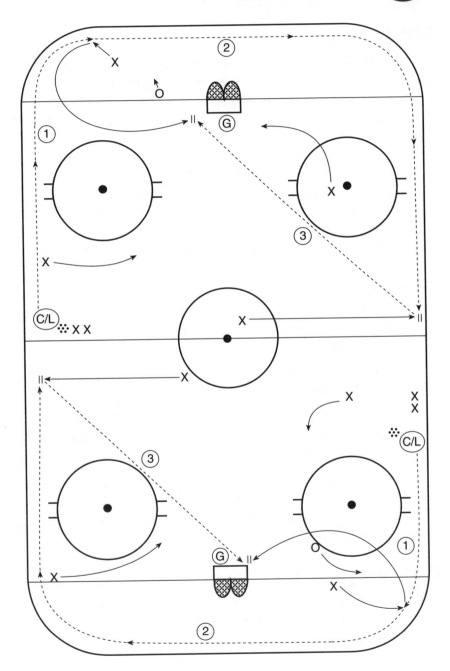

55 SPINNERAMA

Strategy

One way to spread out the defenders is to practice a delay move that buys time for the offense. Do this by changing direction quickly and having the player with the puck travel away from the flow of play. The attacking player with puck possession moves into the opponent's zone, staying wide and looking to go strong to the net for a first option. If the defender has the positional advantage, the puck carrier releases toward the side boards by executing a tight turn or pivot and begins a slow skate along the side wall. This means several players are moving past the puck carrier into the offensive zone, resulting in several passing options.

Procedure

1. Players form groups similar to those in the three-on-two drill previously described (#51) with two defenders entering action once the attack begins.
2. Player behind the net starts the attack and passes to either teammate near the side boards.
3. Puck carrier then straight-line skates down the rink and executes a tight turn near the top of the face-off circle in the opponent's end.
4. Attacking players without the puck skate past the puck carrier and become passing options.
5. If no initial pass is made, players prepare for cycling sequence.

Key Points

- The puck carrier passes the puck after the tight turn only if a teammate is in a prime position to score.
- If an initial pass is not made, take this opportunity to reinforce cycling.
- Add an attacker who jumps into the attack late.

SPINNERAMA 55

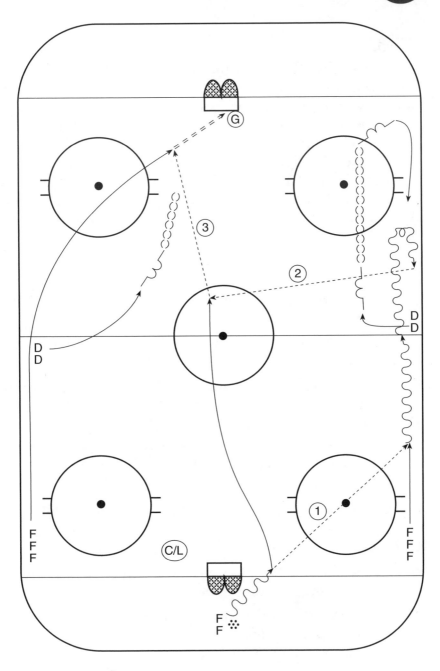

56 SECOND WAVE

Strategy

In this drill, the offensive team has set the puck carrier behind the opponent's net off a dump or cycle. Teammates form an offensive triangle position, each calling for the puck. The player behind the net steps out with the puck, straight-line skates toward the corner of the rink, and hits the defender who arrives through the middle of the zone after a considerable delay. This drill can be executed in a half-rink or full-rink format and may be used in conjunction with the previous drill, Spinnerama (#55), as a way to show various offensive options.

Procedure

1. One attacking player begins with the puck behind the opponent's net.
2. Attackers form a triangle as the puck carrier moves along the end boards.
3. The two players without the puck flash through the prime scoring area in front of the net and call for the puck.
4. The fourth attacker, usually a defensive player for the offensive team, waits in the high slot area just inside the center red line, delays, and then comes late through the middle.
5. The puck carrier delivers a pass and the shot is taken.

Key Points

- Players without the puck move continuously, trying to create openings by forcing defenders to move with them.
- The puck carrier can move back and forth, using the net as protection against defenders.
- The late player reads the situation and jumps into the scoring area at the proper time.

SECOND WAVE 56

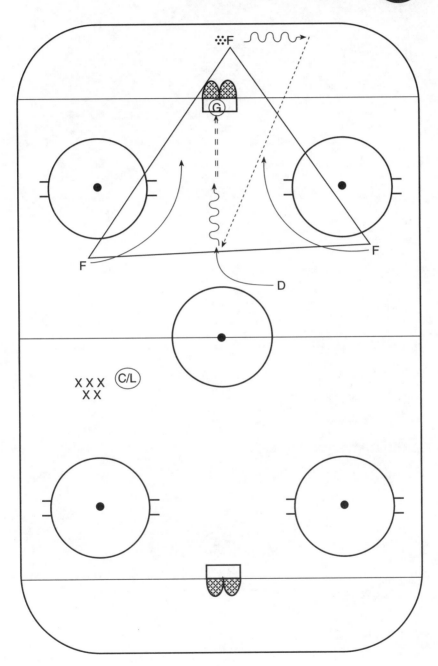

chapter

10

Transition Strategies

In this section our emphasis is on transition play, especially in an attack application, reinforcing the need for players to quickly recognize when to turn from offense to defense or from defense to offense. The three central principles of transition play are these:

- **Principle #1: Accelerate through the mid-rink area.** When moving from defense to offense, players accelerate through the middle of the rink toward the outside boards to receive quick outlet passes.

- **Principle #2: Delay the last player coming back.** The last player leaving the offensive zone should delay and act as an immediate offensive option in case of a turnover.

- **Principle #3: Defend the middle areas first.** When your team moves from offense to defense, players skate toward the middle of the rink.

Good transition play is vital in roller hockey. Whenever a team moves from possessing the puck to defending an opponent or vice versa, some form of transition play takes place. Players who can move into transition at a high tempo give their teams a great advantage—both on the offensive and defensive sides of the puck. Because there are no offsides, a turnover, even from deep in the defensive zone, can quickly be used to set up an attack. Let's look in more detail at the three principles of transition play.

Principle #1: Accelerate Through the Mid-Rink Area

By moving toward the outside areas of the rink, players allow teammates to make safe outlet passes when quickness and surprise are the key elements of success. Mistakes made to the outside of the rink can be more easily defended than those made up the middle, and the boards themselves provide players making an outlet pass with an automatic and relatively safe option, especially when under pressure.

Principle #2: Delay the Last Player Coming Back

When attacking, it is likely that one, two, or sometimes three of your players will end up deep in the opponent's zone. The second principle relates to those players exiting the offensive zone to return to their own end to defend against the other team. When this is occurring, the last player leaving the offensive zone should always be in a position to move back into the attack quickly in case the puck is turned over by the opponent. By trailing the play slightly, the last player can be a dangerous outlet option during a transition play. Also, this player can be designated as the main defender against any second-wave attacks by the opponent as he or she will be perfectly positioned to tie up the late person who tries to enter your zone as a second-wave threat. Many competitive teams designate one of the two defensive players to be a "safety"—someone who is allowed to jump into an offensive attack off a transition play. However, the safety should also be prepared to turn quickly into a defender in the case of a counterattack by the opposition. Often, transition from offense to defense by this designated player is a key component of team success.

Principle #3: Defend the Middle Areas First

Transition can also mean turning from offense to defense. Players should always be concerned with the most dangerous area an opponent can enter—the slot directly in front of the goalie. This is often referred to as the "red" area or "kill" position because so many goals are scored from this location. As a result, teams must be trained to react to their own turnovers by immediately shutting down this important area to their opponents.

Effective transition play, from defense to offense or from attacking to defending, is essential to successful roller hockey play. To be mastered, transition play must be explained, drilled, and continuously reinforced. Without a well-designed transition game, teams will be at a great disadvantage, especially at elite levels.

57 LONG BOMB

Strategy

The first transition drill practices the principle of moving the puck up the rink and into the opponent's zone as quickly as possible. In this play, the opponent has dumped the puck into your zone, perhaps changing players from the bench in the process. The first player back to retrieve the puck gains control and immediately looks to hit a teammate with a long clearing pass. The passer must be sure that the pass is not intercepted and will often be able to use the side boards as a safe outlet area. If the pass is successful, the player goes in for a shot on goal. If the pass misses the mark, the intended receiver attempts to get possession and wait for teammates to gain the zone and provide support.

Procedure

1. Players locate in two equal-sized groups near the top of the face-off circles in opposite corners of the rink.

2. The coach initiates play by directing a puck to the corner, where the goalie retrieves it and sets it for a teammate.

3. The player with the puck sends a long pass up to a player who has entered the play from the other line. The player receiving the pass makes a loop and retrieves the pass off the side boards.

4. Once the attack is completed, the puck is directed into the opposite end for the second goalie to handle, and play proceeds from the opposite end.

Key Points

• The player receiving the pass must be patient and lag behind the play to catch defenders in the wrong zone of the rink.

• The passer makes sure not to give up the puck in the middle area.

LONG BOMB 57

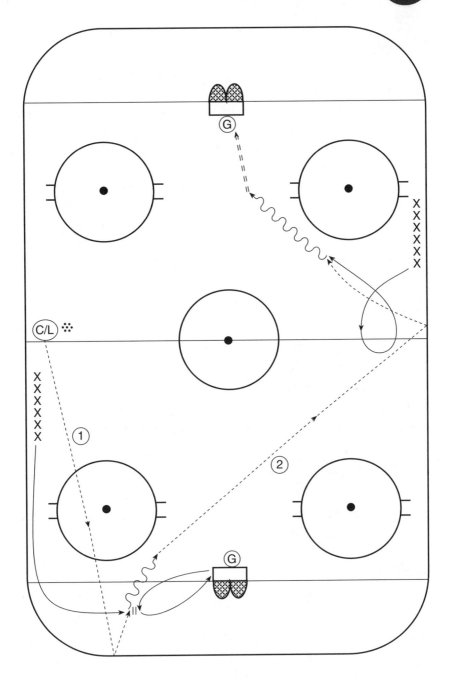

58 SPACE LOB

Strategy

Another way to capitalize on a quick turnover or goalie save is to use the end boards to pass to an area instead of directly to a teammate. In the next drill, the goalie has made a save and a teammate has picked up the loose puck near the front of the net. Rather than carry the puck into the offensive zone he or she attempts to lob it into the far corner of the rink, where a linemate is headed at top speed. This is an excellent way to push the puck up the rink quickly, and often the defensive team will be caught moving in the wrong direction, resulting in an offensive opportunity. Space Lob is a good progression from the previous drill, Long Bomb (#57).

Procedure

1. Players form three groups, two at one end of the rink and the other near the center red line.
2. The coach directs the puck on goalie, who sets it for a circling teammate.
3. As the coach releases the puck on the net, one player from each of the other groups turns up and into the opponent's end at top speed.
4. The puck carrier passes a long pass (or a lob) into the opponent's end.
5. One player retrieves the puck while the others go to the net for a scoring chance.

Key Points

- Players without the puck must see their teammate in control before they move up the rink. This allows for a retreat if a turnover occurs.
- The passer picks a spot in the opponent's zone and tries to lay the puck off the boards for a teammate.

SPACE LOB 58

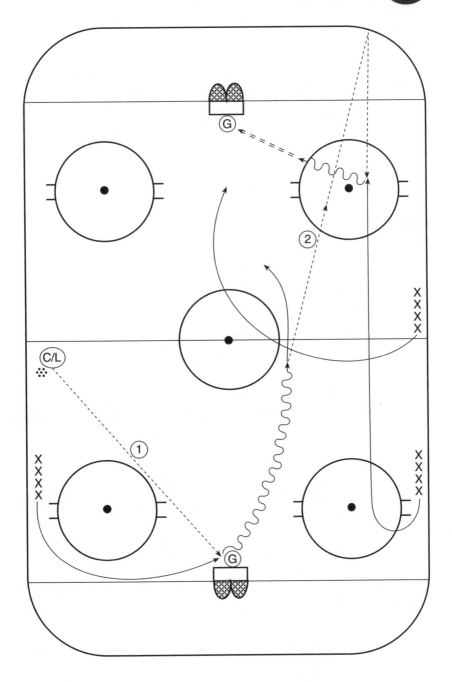

59 THE TRAILER

Strategy

This drill simulates a game situation where a turnover occurs in the middle of the playing surface. Players must move from a retreating position to an attack mode, with one long pass the key to successful transition. Remind players to call for the puck as soon as they see a teammate retrieve a turnover. Also, for the transition to be properly executed, the players without the puck should be in position to be in open passing lanes.

Procedure

1. Forwards form three groups beyond the center red line; defenders group in their defensive end.

2. As the coach soft dumps a puck near the top of the face-off circle in the defensive zone, a defender moves to retrieve it.

3. As the puck is being dumped by the coach, forwards begin skating back toward their own end, with one player lagging behind (a trailer).

4. The defender with the puck sends a long pass off the side boards to the trailing forward, who turns and moves toward the opponent's net for a shot.

Key Points

- Forwards must recognize a transition situation and turn from defense to offense as quickly as they can.

- Forwards who do not receive the pass move toward open areas near the opponent's net for a pass or rebound.

- Defenders work on quick passing, hoping to surprise the opposition.

THE TRAILER 59

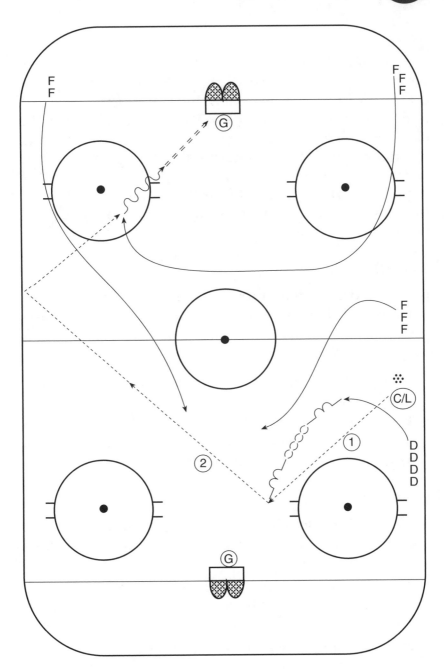

60 SHUTDOWN

Strategy

When shifting from offense to defense, players must contain the most dangerous part of the rink—the middle portion directly in front of the goalie. By regrouping toward the middle area of the playing surface when coming back in a defensive posture, players will force opponents to move into less dangerous scoring positions along the perimeter of the rink. The Shutdown drill emphasizes this defensive positioning to the mid-rink area. This drill is a progression from the previous drill, The Trailer (#59), as the two drills begin with similar group positioning.

Procedure

1. Forwards form three groups in the offensive zone. Defenders group along the side boards near the center red line.
2. The coach begins by directing on a goalie, who relays the puck to a forward cutting behind the net.
3. The puck carrier then dumps the puck deep into the opposite zone to a waiting coach or player.
4. One defender moves into the play and retrieves the puck, while forwards from each group come back into the mid-rink area en route to their defensive coverage.

Key Points

- Players must simulate a defensive situation and look to clog the mid-rink area before entering their own defensive zone.

- The coach who receives the puck gives minimal resistance, only enough to make forwards play defense first before preparing to regroup on offense.

- This is a simple activity for drilling positioning in the defensive zone as a follow-up activity, with players asked to hold positions once the coach gives up the puck.

SHUTDOWN 60

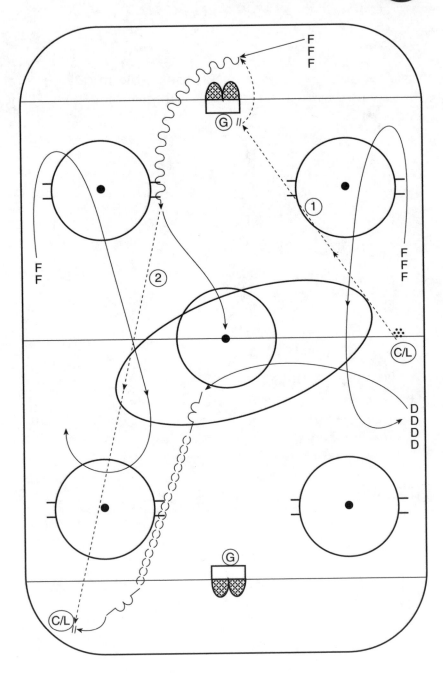

chapter 111

Defensive Team Strategies

How do you defend against an opponent attacking at great speed? A difficult question but one that must be answered if you're to become a proficient roller hockey defender. In this section we'll highlight some of the principles inherent to defensive tactics and provide drills designed to sharpen defensive skills.

- **Principle #1: Force opponents outside.** Attempt to limit your opponent to the outside portions of the rink.

- **Principle #2: Do not commit too soon.** When defending, don't overcommit or turn to defend too quickly, as recovery is difficult at high speed.

- **Principle #3: Maintain proper skate alignment.** Align your skates in the same direction that the opposing offensive player is headed.

Many coaches believe the defensive side of the game is easier to teach than the offensive side. The defensive aspect of the game is similar to offense and transition play in that some basic principles must be adhered to in order to maximize the success of defensive strategies and tactics. Here's more of what you need to know about these principles:

Principle #1: Force Opponents Outside

Depending on skill levels, the game of roller hockey can be played at a very fast pace, which makes defending difficult, especially when you're outnumbered. Players may not initially be in position to take the puck away from an opponent as they enter the defensive zone. However, the defensive players must attempt to limit their opponents from prime goal-scoring positions traditionally associated with the middle portions of the ice. In forcing the opponent to the outside areas of the playing surface, you deny easy access to the goal. Players should consistently position themselves so as to defend the mid-rink territory and force opposing players to the outside lanes.

Principle #2: Do Not Commit Too Soon

Unless a player is 100% certain he or she can attack and retrieve the puck while defending, it's better to hold your position and be patient. Why? Because once a player commits to an attack in the defensive zone, it is difficult to recover if the decision turns out to be a poor one. The results can be fatal, especially against a skilled opponent who can take advantage of the extended recovery time that is almost inevitable in roller hockey and advance into a prime scoring location before the defender can react. Players must learn to read situations quickly and use anticipation before committing to defend an offensive player.

Principle #3: Maintain Proper Skate Alignment

While this sounds simple, it often is not, especially when you're defending a gifted offensive opponent. This principle highlights the importance of positioning in defensive play. If a defending player is positioned to match an opponent stride for stride toward the goal area, his or her chances for a successful defense are much better. However, whenever a defender changes direction continuously and uses tight pivots and turns to pursue an opponent, the attacking player gains an advantage.

Given the emphasis on offensive play that the rules and dynamics of the game create, defending in roller hockey can be difficult for even highly skilled players. Work on drills and activities that reinforce basic defensive proficiency. The drills in this chapter will help players develop these basics; the emphasis is on preventing goals and defending territory using either a passive or attacking defense. There are advantages and disadvantages to each type of defensive coverage, and the skill level of your team should determine the type of coverage you employ. While roller hockey emphasizes offensive play, before you can play offense you must possess the puck. Good defense helps a team create turnovers and gain possession, the first condition of successful offensive play. Without sound defensive principles, planning, and practice, roller hockey can be a difficult enterprise indeed!

61 CONTAIN TO CORNER

Strategy

Just as a full-rink one-on-one drill can hone offensive skills, as seen in earlier chapters, many of the drills for offensive and transition play can reinforce defensive technique, as well. When assuming the role of a defending player, keep the shoulder closest to the rink boards squarely in the midline body area of the attacking player. By keeping your shoulder in the midline area you ensure solid positioning to defend against the sudden change of direction or shift in speed that your opponent will surely attempt. Coaches can design practice for defensive players to receive more one-on-one time by emphasizing half-rink over full-rink drills. This increases the number of repetitions for any given period, as seen in this drill.

Procedure

1. Four pairs of forwards locate on either side of the center red line, two on each side of the rink. Defenders position in the center face-off circle.
2. Both sides begin at the whistle with a forward passing a puck to the opposite forward line, looping, and then receiving the puck back. The forward then skates back toward the end where play initiated for a shot on goal.
3. At the same time, the defenders skate around the center face-off circle, pivot to backward skating, and defend against the oncoming forward.
4. Defenders attempt to force forwards into the outside areas of the zone and contain toward the corners, never allowing any cutbacks to the mid-rink area.

Key Points

- Defensive players can give space to the outside, inviting the forward to take it.
- Depending on the speed of the attacker, the defender may not have time to pivot. If defending while skating forward, take the opportunity to work at angling.

CONTAIN TO CORNER 61

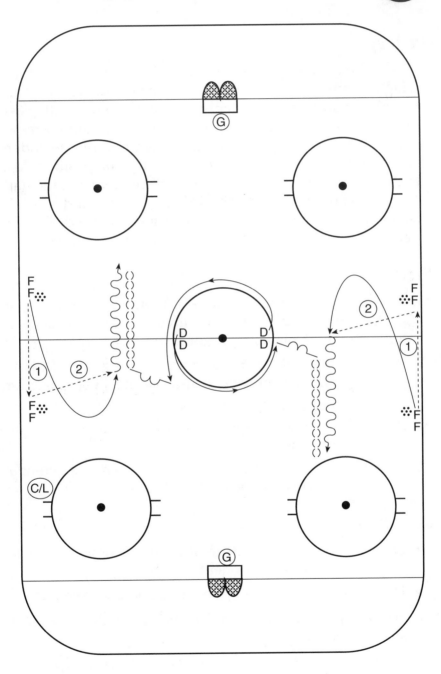

62 GAP CONTROL

Strategy

One of the most important defensive concepts is "gapping," which is controlling the space between yourself as a defending player and an attacking opponent. When an offensive player has a large gap, he or she usually has more time to operate and exploit the defense. So, when possible, defenders should anticipate where the puck is headed and position close to the opponent receiving the puck, thus reducing the gap. This will cause unforced errors and turnovers and possibly lead to transition opportunities. This gap control drill trains players to step up and efficiently reduce time and space.

Procedure

1. Players split into four groups, one in each corner of the rink. Each group consists of two lines, one defensive and one offensive, with players alternating turns out of each corner.

2. The defensive player follows a puck carrier and pivots from forward to backward skating in whichever direction the puck carrier travels.

3. The defensive player attempts to play a one-on-one while maintaining a tight gap.

4. Play is finished when either a shot is taken or a defender clears the puck; then the next pair begins.

Key Points

- Defensive players keep as small a gap as possible between themselves and the opponent.
- Defenders focus on the opponent's body, not the puck.
- To force quick feet, start the drill with both players on their knees or bellies.
- Add a second turn by the offensive player to force the defender to change the gap twice during the activity.

GAP CONTROL 62

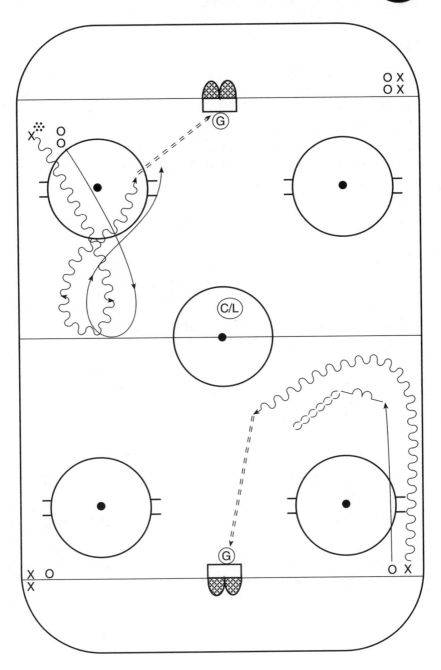

63 LOCK-UP

Strategy

When they can, defensive players should position themselves so that their coverages are easier to identify and execute. Through keeping the in-line skates properly positioned, the chances for success increase. Roller hockey is an exceptionally quick game, with angles of attack and defense changing constantly. A minor mistake in defensive positioning can lead to a goal-scoring opportunity for the opponent. This drill forces defenders to lock on one attacking opponent while maintaining similar speed and direction.

Procedure

1. Players form two equal-sized groups, one along either side board.
2. One group attacks while the other group defends.
3. Three attackers leave the boards and go anywhere they choose; the coach passes a puck to one of the attackers.
4. As the pass is completed, three defenders lock on to one opponent each in their defensive zone.

Key Points

- The defenders try to prevent the attackers from getting any shots on goal.
- Emphasize positioning and enforce locking on one player only.
- Add another line of players to be late-arriving backcheckers who assist in the defensive zone.

LOCK-UP 63

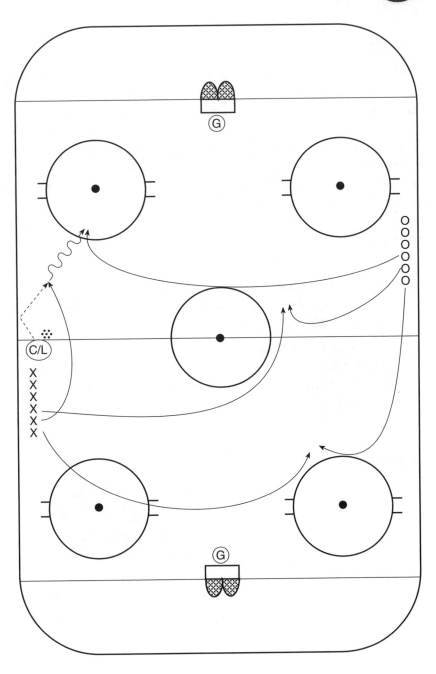

64 STATIC BOX

Strategy

This drill incorporates a simple static box defense with players given specific responsibilities depending on the puck's location. The defending team's emphasis is to force shots from outside and deny any penetration into the red or kill area in front of the goalie. The defending team attempts to gain possession of the puck through an errant pass or shot on goal from the opponent. This passive defensive system is similar to a zone defense you see in basketball.

Procedure

1. Players form equal-sized groups; half play offense and half assume defensive roles at one end of the rink. Groups switch assignments after each attempt. Extra players wait with the coach for their turn.
2. Defenders cannot attack the offensive players but must wait in a static or box formation with minimal movement while attempting to deny offensive opportunities.
3. Offensive players attempt to penetrate the box for quality scoring chances.

Key Points

- Defenders practice patience and learn which shots to allow—for example, from long range or a bad angle.
- Defenders look weak side (over their shoulder) so that attackers do not gain a favorable position.
- Defenders focus on placing their sticks in passing lanes to deny offensive access.
- This drill can be done with no sticks for the defending players, giving an emphasis to body position.
- Try adding a second puck.

STATIC BOX 64

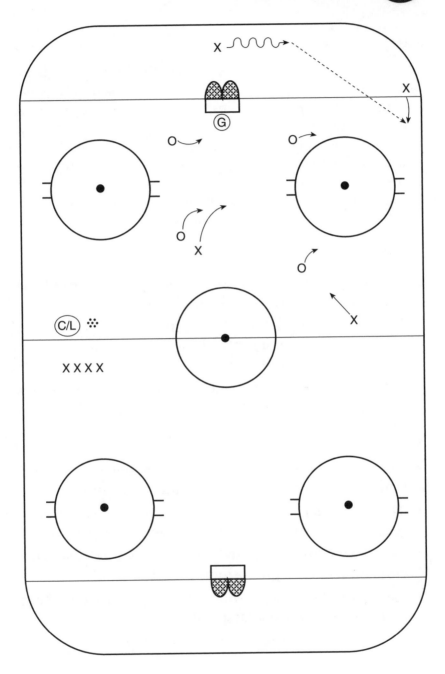

65 TRIANGLE PLUS ONE

Strategy

Another form of passive coverage is called the "triangle plus one." This coverage is designed to congest the middle area of the zone and force an attacking opponent to stay outside. The three top players form a triangle, always fronting the opponent with the puck and forcing passes away from the mid-rink area. The low person (the "plus one") tries to prevent any goal-mouth passes and directs the puck to teammates if a turnover occurs. This defensive formation can be very effective for creating transition opportunities.

Procedure

1. The defensive team positions against four opponents who are allowed to go anywhere in the zone.

2. Whenever the puck goes low, the "plus one" player is allowed to move and attack, with the triangle shifting while keeping formation.

3. When the puck goes out high, defending players hold their positions and attempt to force long-range shots.

Key Points

- The players in the triangle remain patient and hold position, remembering this is not an attack defense.

- The low player is prepared to move toward any player who sets up in front of the goalie for potential screen shots.

- For a variation, practice with no sticks for defensive players with the focus on positioning.

- Generally, the three defending forwards form the triangle, and the defensive player is the "one."

TRIANGLE PLUS ONE 65

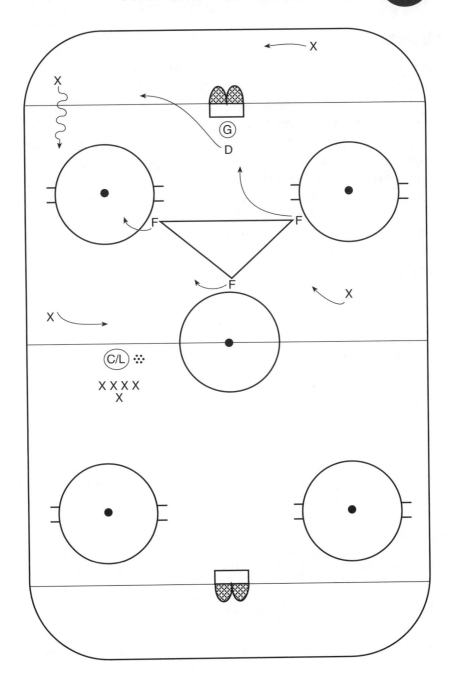

66 THE DIAMOND

Strategy

Some teams employ a more aggressive defensive scheme where defenders attack the puck carrier to force turnovers. This drill incorporates a "diamond defense," or a 1-2-1, that looks similar to the triangle plus one defense just described. The main difference in this defense is that the defending players are much more active and depend on each other to cover areas of the defensive zone if one of the players decides to attack. This defensive strategy is similar to a zone coverage in basketball, with players changing location in the diamond to deal with specific situations as they arise. This type of coverage requires tremendous trust among teammates and a great amount of practice to perfect.

Procedure

1. Four defenders establish a diamond position in the defensive zone, with four attackers positioned anywhere in the zone.
2. The coach begins play by directing a puck to any of the attacking players.
3. One defender then forces the puck carrier while the remaining defensive players read and react, depending on where the puck is passed.
4. Play continues until the goalie makes a save or the puck is cleared by the defending team.

Key Points

- Defenders anticipate and move quickly to break up offensive formations.
- Defenders shift and cover for a teammate attacking the puck carrier, remembering to protect the red zone or slot area.
- The concept of "head on a swivel" should be reinforced for defensive players, who are always looking over their shoulders for attacking players coming from the weak side.

THE DIAMOND 66

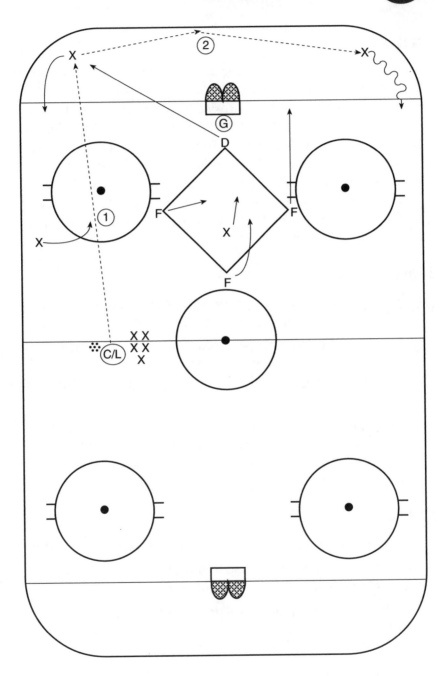

67 TWO-ON-TWO LOW

Strategy

Whichever type of defensive coverage a team elects to use, it's vital that all players learn basic one-on-one skills in their defensive zone so that coverages will succeed. Previous drills have practiced one-on-one activities against opponents attacking with speed. The next two drills reinforce one-on-one play in a defensive posture given to "hand-to-hand combat" along the boards. Both drills emphasize the need to develop a good sense of where your opponent is at all times, with or without the puck. Through two-on-two down low drilling, players gain physical conditioning and defensive awareness.

Procedure

1. Two players are on offense and two on defense playing below the tops of the face-off circles in either zone.

2. The two offensive players take their positions and retrieve a puck dumped to a corner by the coach. As the attackers attempt to score, the defensive players try to restrict quality chances.

3. The drill is completed when the puck is in the net, smothered by the goalie, or cleared from the area by the defenders. Four fresh players then begin in the other corner for a new sequence.

Key Points

- Players work to develop man-to-man defending skills.
- Add one player on offense to make the drill a three-on-two exercise, allowing for more offense.
- Add a defender (two-on-three) to increase defensive pressure.

TWO-ON-TWO LOW

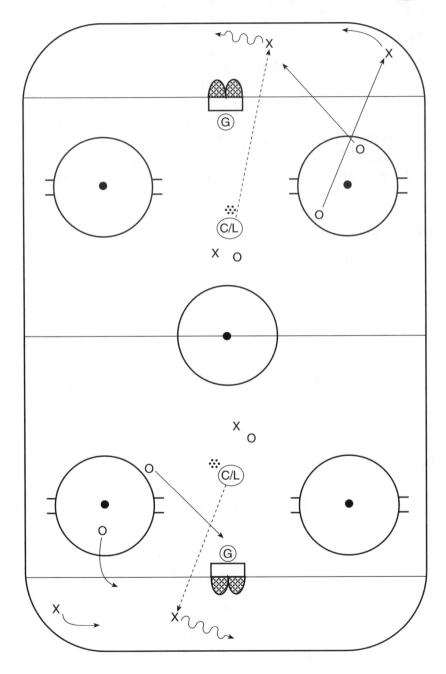

68 THREE-ON-THREE LOW

Strategy

This is a natural progression from Two-on-Two Low. Defenders play either a passive or attack system, remembering to protect the slot area against dangerous offensive opportunities. This drill can be run half-rink or full-rink. On the full-rink, defenders, once they get possession of the puck, attempt a transition break into the other end. The drill then continues with players switching from offense to defense and vice versa.

Procedure

1. Play may occur anywhere below the tops of the face-off circles, thereby restricting space and emphasizing defensive low work.
2. The three defenders begin by assuming their positions, lying on their bellies. A coach begins the drill by giving the puck to one of the three offensive players.
3. The attacking players can start from any offensive area they choose.
4. Play ends at the whistle, and another group begins fresh.

Key Points

- The defensive players attempt to stay in a triangle formation rather than all three defending the puck carrier simultaneously.
- Defenders may choose to immediately engage opponents man-to-man.
- Remind defenders to look over their shoulders for attackers advancing from behind them.
- To focus on defensive positioning, defenders can work with no sticks or with sticks turned upside down.

THREE-ON-THREE LOW

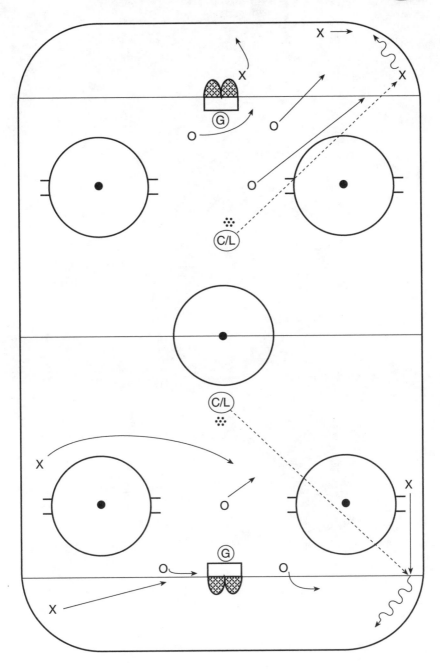

chapter

12

Game Performance Tips

Coaches and players are always looking for strategies, equipment, or ideas that might give them a competitive edge. With this in mind, we'll conclude our look at roller hockey with some suggestions on how to improve performance so that you'll always be at the top of your game. Following is a Top 10 list of ideas to improve your play. Although many of these suggestions are simple and easy to implement, when taken together they'll play a significant role in improving performance. As roller hockey evolves into the next century, both equipment and tactics will continue to improve. Undoubtedly, you'll be able to add your own ideas to this list of tips as you grow along with the game.

When You're Outsized by an Opponent, Outthink the Opponent!

There is always somebody bigger, stronger, or faster to compete against. Given the nature of roller hockey, a lack of size can actually be an advantage. If you do find yourself up against a physically imposing opponent, remember a few simple tips:

• Use quickness through turning and pivoting to reduce the impact of size. They can't stop what they can't catch!

• Make yourself big along the boards by spreading out your arms and using the tops of the boards for balance. You may not be big, but you'll seem big if you use the boards to your advantage in tight situations.

• Keep your feet moving as much as possible. This creates momentum, and momentum is tough to stop, even for the biggest of opponents. When contact is made, a smaller player can actually have a physical advantage because of speed at the point of attack.

Smaller players often enjoy an advantage over larger opponents in maneuverability and quickness.

Monitor Shift Times for Maximum Efficiency

Depending on the skill of your opponent, your physical conditioning, and the environment you're playing in, the length of time you will play each time on the rink (commonly known as "shift time") should vary. If you're playing against an overmatched opponent, shift times might exceed 60 seconds, as your efforts will not be as exhausting. However, more skilled adversaries will demand more effort, resulting in shift times ranging from 35 to 50 seconds. Players and coaches should recognize this important aspect of game performance to maximize both effort and outcome.

Drink Plenty of Fluids While Playing

As roller hockey is often played under very hot conditions, it's important to stay hydrated. If you're outdoors or in an arena without air conditioning, you'll lose an enormous amount of water during a game. Hydrate often during games—and don't wait until you feel thirsty, as that might be too late. As a general rule, you should drink small amounts of liquid each time you come off from a shift and are resting on the bench. As you gain experience, you'll know better how much liquid you need to drink during a game. There's no hard and fast rule about this.

Know Your Strengths and Use Them!

Roller hockey is predominantly a skill game, and speed is a key component. Remember this when developing your skills or when selecting a team as part of a management group. However, we can't be all things to all people, and some players will simply never become roller hockey speed-burners. Decide what you can bring to your team and then bring it! With practice, you'll be able to improve other aspects of your play, but this will take time. If you're managing or coaching a team, consider having some players focus primarily on defense. We recommend that at least four players per squad be trained defenders. While the tactics of the sport are based in offense, and it is easy for alleged defensive players to get caught up in rushing the puck or joining the attack, there remains a need for defensive awareness and commitment.

Generate Speed Through the Middle of the Rink

Picking up speed in the center of the rink allows you to move quickly into scoring position or to retreat into defense. Avoid coasting or standing still, as the dynamics of the game demand quick movement in all phases. The middle area of the rink is expansive and can be used as a launching pad to get up to maximum speed. As the play moves from defense to offense, prepare to come through the middle and sling shot hard toward the side boards on your way into the offensive zone.

Eliminate the Give-and-Go by Closing Down the Passing Lanes

Because contact is not encouraged in most roller leagues, it's important to eliminate your opponent's passing opportunities by positioning players in passing lanes. Don't allow opponents to create options by using give-and-go tactics. As a defender, try to move into a position that will prevent a player from receiving a return pass. Although this will be affected to some degree by what type of defensive coverage you're using, the principle is a good one.

Use Picks and Screens in the Offensive Zone

While interference is a penalty, proper legal positioning can create difficult situations for an opponent to fight through. Make sure players understand the concept behind any screen plays before they are attempted, and always play within the rules. Screening the goalie, for example, is one way to maximize shooting opportunities by forcing the goalie to hunt for the puck. On offense, roller hockey often resembles a faster game of basketball, with half-court set plays the order of the day. If properly employed, screens and picks can create tremendous scoring opportunities.

Eliminate Opposition Speed Players Through the Middle

The difficulty of quick pivots or turns, especially for defending players, makes it important that the opponent not be allowed to generate great speed through the middle of the rink. Work at picking up potentially dangerous players before they can attack at full speed.

Work for Quality Scoring Chances and Eliminate Shots From Far Out

A defender shooting the puck on net from long range is not a high percentage shot in roller hockey. Work for grade-A shots, or look for tip-ins or redirects. You want to make goalies move from side to side in this game because such movements are difficult for them to do. Shots from long range will not accomplish this.

Give Considerable Thought to Special Teams Play

Whether it's a four-on-three, four-on-two, three-on-two, or any other special teams situation, remember that control is the key to effective play. Players should move toward "quiet zones" such as behind the opposition net or off to the side where they will attract less attention from an opponent. This will allow for quick release of a shot and rebound opportunities, both keys to power-play success.

Roller hockey is a dynamic game that people of most ages and across many skill levels can enjoy. By understanding the major principles and concepts of play described throughout this book, you'll increase both your skills and your love of the game.

Good luck—and keep your stick on the pavement!

Sample Practice Plans

This section highlights the keys to structuring a successful practice and provides some sample practice sessions using drills from the book.

- **Take time to prepare.** Have a general game plan for each practice session and share the objectives for that specific practice with players beforehand. Most players want to improve and please their coaches but find it difficult to do either if they do not understand what is expected of them.

- **Use the entire roller surface efficiently.** Rather than running all full-rink drills, split the surface in halves, thirds, or even quarters. Make every second count toward skill development during practice.

- **Break the team into workable groups.** To keep players active during practice, break the team into small groups or pairs so that players can be involved at the same times and can repeat each drill if time allows.

- **Consider station work to reinforce specific skills.** Divide the team into groups with each group at its own drill station. The number of stations you use will depend on the number of players practicing, time per station, intensity of activity, and so on.

- **A drill from one topic area can often easily be used during another part of practice.** For example, a three-on-three drill done at a slower speed can be used as a warm-up. Experiment with different combinations and request feedback about how effective a practice was on a given day. The perfect practice might be just around the corner!

Important Notes

- In the following sample practice sessions, "Total Activity Time" does *not* include transition time between drills or time for water breaks.

- Precede every practice with a simple stretching routine (see chapter 3).

SAMPLE PRACTICE PLAN 1

Total Time:
60 minutes

Theme:
Team Passing and Transition Play

Objective:
To refine general passing skills while establishing a high tempo during transition

Drill Sequence	**Time Required** (min)
1. Drill 6—Long Figure 8 *An effective loosening up activity to get the blood flowing*	4
2. Drill 9—Puck Control Warm-Up *Relaxes the arms and hands in preparation for passing activities to follow*	6
3. Drill 19—Partner Pass *A simple introduction to passing and receiving*	8
4. Drill 20—Line Pass *Add shots at the end to warm up goalies*	6
5. Drill 22—Russian Wheel *A high tempo, skill-oriented activity; finish drill with shots for goalies*	8
6. Drill 57—Long Bomb *A transition drill for accurate passing while using the boards*	6
7. Drill 59—The Trailer *Work on quick outlet transition*	10
8. Drill 52—Cycling *Finish the practice with a fun activity that also conditions*	6
9. Recap, optional skate at the end, or free time.	6
Total Activity Time	**60**

SAMPLE PRACTICE PLAN 2

Total Time:
60 minutes

Theme:
Puck Control

Objective:
To reinforce puck control skills in game-related environments

Drill Sequence	Time Required (min)
1. Drill 1—Snake *Use this drill as a warm-up to work on knee-bend and leg extension*	5
2. Drill 3—The Loop *Helps to develop turning skills while controlling the puck.*	5
3. Drill 11—Pylon Madness *Work on keeping the head up and looking out, not down*	6
4. Drill 15—Face the Music *This drill conditions, too*	4
5. Drill 17—Puck Control Shinney *Players enjoy this activity that improves puck control in tight situations*	10
6. Drill 32—Center Pivots *Provides shots for goalies to keep them involved and sharp*	6
7. Drill 36—Red Line Down *Forces players to develop puck control skills under pressure*	6
8. Drill 47—Center Scramble *Players like this variation on scrimmaging*	8
9. Showdown (one-on-one with goalie from center rink) *A great way to finish any practice*	5
10. Free time to work on individual skills	5

Total Activity Time	**60**

SAMPLE PRACTICE PLAN 3

Total Time:
60 minutes

Theme:
Individual and Team Defense

Objective:
To develop individual defending skills within the context of a team system

Drill Sequence	Time Required (min)
1. Drill 2—Three Up and Out *Warm up with an easy skate to begin practice*	4
2. Drill 5—Backward Clear *Reinforces the need to pivot and skate backward*	3
3. Drill 40—Rapid Fire *Allows goalies to feel the puck early in practice*	6
4. Drill 16—Off the Hip *Players practice puck control one-on-one*	4
5. Drill 14—The Rabbit *Combines skating, intensity, and defense*	8
6. Drill 37—Hitch a Ride *Game-like situation that requires second effort*	6
7. Drill 61—Contain to Corner *Works on individual angling skills*	5
8. Drill 50—Two-on-One Attack *Defending player must make good decisions*	5
9. Drill 67—Two-on-Two Low *Forces players to maintain defensive positioning*	8
10. Drill 64—Static Box *Works team defense within a particular style of play*	8
11. Cool down and stretch *Recap key teaching points during this time together*	3

Total Activity Time   **60**

about the authors

Dave Easter

K. Vern Stenlund

Dave Easter knows what it takes to teach winning roller hockey. Currently the Manager of In-Line Hockey for the Canadian Hockey Association, he coached the Men's Canadian National In-Line Team to silver medals in the 1995 and 1996 World Championships and also helped steer the junior team to a gold medal in the 1996 World Championships.

An NCCP (National Coaching Certification Program) Advanced Level Hockey Coach, Easter also coached in the Western Junior B Ice Hockey League in Ontario, Canada, for five years and served as coaching coordinator for the Chatham Minor League Hockey Association in 1994. He has coached the Men's In-Line National Team as part of his participation in the Canadian Hockey Association (CHA) Program of Excellence, the organization's in-line equivalent of its enormously successful ice hockey program.

Easter is a member of the Canadian Hockey Association and the Canadian Professional Coaching Association. An internationally respected ambassador of roller hockey, Easter also has been invited on several occasions to teach the sport in Australia.